The German Cinema

Roger Manvell
and
Heinrich Fraenkel

The German Cinema

PRAEGER PUBLISHERS
New York · Washington

BOOKS THAT MATTER
Published in the United States of America in 1971
by Praeger Publishers, Inc., 111 Fourth Avenue,
New York, N.Y. 10003

Library of Congress Catalog Card Number: 71–143490

Printed in Great Britain

Contents

Illustrations

ERRATUM

In the plates caption 80 refers to the lower picture and caption 81 refers to the upper picture.

Authors' preface

In the comparatively brief space available to us in this book we attempt to give a succinct and objective account of the main phases through which the German cinema has passed from the early, pioneer period at the turn of the century to the present day, when new movements, mainly among the younger film-makers, may be able to restore Germány once again to its previous high status in world cinema.

With considerations of space in mind, we have selected certain outstanding or otherwise important films for somewhat longer treatment than the rest. Germany's vast output, especially since 1920, inevitably demands fairly drastic selection, but when works are especially representative of a trend in style, such as *The Cabinet of Dr Caligari* or *Kameradschaft*, or of historical or social importance, such as *Triumph of the Will, Ohm Krüger*, or *The Eternal Jew*, we felt justified in giving them the space they occupy, even including in a few instances detailed annotations of their continuity. In the case of many films not easy to come by we have indicated their plots; nothing is more irritating than to read comments on films in which the basic story or situation is not made clear. This is especially true for younger readers who have not had the opportunity to see the so-called classics of the German cinema.

Lastly, we feel we should state our own position in relation to the interpretation of German cinema. In our view there has been a tendency to over-interpret the silent film before Hitler, especially in the case of the so-called expressionist films. We do not want to under-estimate the dedicated work of Siegfried Kracauer, who was known personally to both of us, but we believe his book *From Caligari to Hitler* greatly exaggerates the significance of many of the films about which he writes, and so distorts through over-emphasis what is no doubt a partial truth in his arguments. Lotte

Eisner, we believe, in her book *L'Ecran Démoniaque*, offers a more balanced approach to the macabre and expressionist German cinema, about which our own views will be found in Chapter Two. These films, though often impressive and beautiful, are, we think, less 'significant', both socially and psychologically, than they have been made to seem.

We hope that this book will be of some use in bringing together certain of the principal facts about the German cinema, and in offering an objective assessment of the worth of some of the principal films to have been made in Germany while quoting, when they seemed relevant or helpful, the views of others. We think, too, that our account of the film industry during the Nazi period, when propaganda was, with careful calculation, restricted to only a comparatively few 'prestige' films, is correct in its emphasis.

ROGER MANVELL and HEINRICH FRAENKEL
1970

Acknowledgments

The Authors would like to acknowledge the invaluable help they have received from G. Buckland-Smith, Lutz Becker, the National Film Archive Stills Department, and, in Germany, the assistance of Herren Fürstenau and Spiess of the Deutsches Institut für Filmkunde, and of Herr Klaue of the GDR Film-Archive. In Berlin, we received help from Kinemathek and in London from Clive Coultass of the Imperial War Museum. To all, we tender our thanks, and also to Mrs Enid Audus for her secretarial assistance in helping us prepare both the script and the illustrations for the press. For additional advice we should like to thank Felix Bucher and Dieter Geissler.

Chapter one

Pioneers in a new art 1895-1918

The origins of the cinema, like the initial displays of moving pictures on the screen, were significantly international. However much chauvinistic prejudice and financial interests were to attempt later to divide the cinema into its various national components, its fundamental internationalism has remained apparent from the period of the pioneers to the present day. In the case of Germany, it was Oskar Messter [1] who contributed the Maltese cross to the projector and, unlike other pioneers such as Edison, the Sklada-nowskys and the Lumières, believed the cinema to have a future and made it his life's career. While the Lumières' agents were making and showing the early 'occasional' films, which recorded any subject available in cities throughout the world (in Britain, in the United States, and even the coronation procession of Tsar Nikolai II in Moscow in May 1896), the first indigenous German films were being demonstrated at home. The first public screening in Germany by Max and Emil Skladanowsky [2] had actually preceded that of the Lumières in Paris; their Bioskop show opened on 1st November 1895 at the Berlin music-hall, the Wintergarten; the Lumières showed their films for the first time to the public two months later, on 28th December at the Grand Café, Boulevard des Capuchines.

Messter became Germany's first, and principal, pioneer producer. He began in 1897 in a small studio on the Friedrichstrasse in Berlin. Like all those who contributed to the establishment of the film as a permanent entertainment industry, he poured out hundreds of short films at the turn of the century, most of them little more than movie squibs, the sole importance of which was that they introduced motion pictures to the public. By 1900 most of the major cities of the world had had the opportunity of seeing such films (news stories, brief 'documentaries' or 'interest' films, vaudeville turns, primitive stories and jokes, trick films demonstrating the 'magic' of the camera, and so forth) in their music-halls, in fair-grounds, in empty premises temporarily converted into show-places for programmes lasting from a few minutes to half an hour. A typical film of 1897 was:

AT THE CARD TABLE: Two gentlemen seated in a garden are expecting a friend for a game of cards. He arrives, and they welcome him with pleasure while a pretty maid serves brandy. Then a dis-agreement occurs about the game; one of the gentlemen, very excited, reaches for the garden-hose and squirts water at his friend, who protects himself by opening his umbrella.

'This was supposed to be funny,' said Messter forty years later, 'our standards were modest.' But he made many recordings of historical importance, such as shots of the Kaiser at Stettin in 1897, and Bismarck in his retirement. Also he began the practice of using artificial lighting before any other producer.

As his productions became somewhat more ambitious after 1900, he introduced on the silent screen—as other pioneer producers were to do in Britain, the United States and France—famous stars from cabaret and music-hall, such as Otto Reuter, who mingled bitter-ness with humour, and Robert Steidl. They mouthed their way through familiar songs and stage routines before the camera, but as the films were either accompanied by 'live' music in the vaudeville theatres, or were covered by a commentator assisted by a gramo-phone in the 'shop cinemas' which began to be popular from 1904, the absence of the voices of these vocalists seemed to matter less than might at first appear. This was a period when established stars had to be persuaded to appear before the cameras—one re-members D. W. Griffith's shame at having to accept work as a motion picture actor in 1907. Messter, however, like the producers of the *film d'arte* movement in Italy and the *film d'art* in France, was determined to raise the status, if not the actual artistic standard of the subjects he filmed, and in 1908 he presented the actor Giam-petro, then a star of international fame from the Metropol Theater. Messter, again like others, experimented with synchronized sound, using the phonograph. The main problem here was not so much the quality of the sound as the absence of any means of amplification. However, as early as 1903 Messter produced a film with Steidl called *On the Cycle Track*, with a comic narration by the comedian. Giampetro also appeared in a film produced by Alfred Duskes, *Don Juan Gets Married* (*Don Juan Heiratet*). Duskes, who was previously involved in film exhibition, was later to become Messter's partner.

Messter, of course, was not alone. By 1910 dozens of film companies were producing short films, but the import of foreign products was as easy as the export of the films made in Germany. Gradually a few of the German companies drew ahead of the rest because of the scale, and in some cases the quality, of their output. Prints were still bought and sold outright, not hired. Foreign companies such as Pathé and Eclair had centres in Germany. The more prominent German firms were Projektions A. G. Union of Frankfurt and Messter's company, now Messter and Duskes. The first International Cinematographic Industry Exhibition was held in Hamburg in June 1908, and Charles Urban of Britain demonstrated Kinemacolor, the newly patented British colour process developed by his partner, George Albert Smith, in a Berlin music-hall in 1909. The industry was getting under way, and Germany, like other countries, was now to move on to a fully developed form of film entertainment by establishing cinemas from around 1908,[3] in which much longer, rented films were soon to be shown, which offered the public the first stages towards full-length feature entertainment. Messter's first *Grossfilm* (long film) was made in 1909; this was *Andreas Hofer*, a film about the Tyrolean folk-hero of the Napoleonic period, directed by Carl Froelich,[4] and filmed on location in the Tyrol itself.

The period following 1910 saw attempts in several countries to bring to the screen an increasing number of famous actors and actresses. As the story-films lengthened, help from the theatre seemed to be essential, partly because the films themselves were growing more complex in their form and subject and partly because producers wanted to raise the social level of their audiences, increasing the admission charges in order to meet their rising costs. For example, in Italy the rights to d'Annunzio's works were acquired for the screen; in France actors from the Comédie Française, even the great Sarah Bernhardt herself, were hired to gesticulate their way through the well-known plots of such plays as *The Lady of the Camellias*. In Britain Sir Johnston Forbes-Robertson appeared in a full-length film version of *Hamlet*, reconstructing the action from his stage production, but adding location scenes shot in Cornwall. In Germany, however, the Association of Berlin Theatre Directors refused in 1912 to allow any stage actors to appear in films; but the ban was disregarded. In 1912 the director Max Mack [5] brought the great German actor Albert Bassermann [6] to the screen in an adaptation of Paul Lindau's successful stage play *The Other One* (*Der Andere*). It was the first film to be criticized seriously in the press. Lindau received the equivalent of £25 for the screen rights to his play, which had a Jekyll-and-Hyde theme, featuring a Berlin lawyer played by Bassermann, who was at first very dubious about the whole thing. Mack, though still very young, had the courage to 'coach' the great actor, who was already in his forties and giving at the time a remarkable performance in *Othello* at Reinhardt's Deutsches Theater. Instead of openly instructing him in screen acting in front of the studio technicians, Mack let him record a highly theatrical scene from *Othello*. He then sent everyone away except the cameraman and one electrician, and spent two hours rehearsing the actor in a modified, more cinematic style of performance in the same scene. He then filmed this second test scene, and showed Bassermann both versions. The actor was intrigued by the result, and his initial doubts about appearing on the screen were resolved. Another actor at the Deutsches Theater was the still unknown Ernst Lubitsch, aged eighteen.

Der Andere was one of the first of the so-called *Autorenfilm* (famous writer films) on which those film-makers who wanted to raise the standard of the cinema began to concentrate. Max Mack was among these, commissioning a comedy from the dramatist Franz von Schoenthan, *Where is Coletti?* (*Wo ist Coletti?*, 1912, with Madge Lessing). Established books were adapted for the screen, such as *The Vow of Stefan Huller* (1912), from a best-seller by Felix Holländer. Films were made from Schiller (*Don Carlos* in 1910), and from Schnitzler (*Liebelei*, a Danish production, in 1914). Even the great Max Reinhardt descended from the stage to the studio and let his pantomime *Sumurun* be filmed in 1910, an exact replica of the stage production. The emphasis was on culture at the price of the natural growth of the cinema, the roots of which could scarcely expand in the heavy soil of literature and the drama.

4

The following year Paul Wegener [7] made his first appearance on the screen in the film which remains by title (the film itself is not preserved) the best-known German production of the pre-war period, *The Student of Prague* (*Der Student von Prag*, 1913). Approaching the age of forty, the actor was fascinated by the artistic possibilities in the cinema for creating the atmosphere of the supernatural, and he took especial care in preparing this film himself, working with the writer Hanns Heinz Ewers (in later years to script the notorious Nazi film, *Horst Wessel*) on ideas for the action collectively derived (as Siegfried Kracauer has pointed out) from Hoffmann, Poe's *William Wilson*, the legend of *Faust* and Oscar Wilde. The director, Stellan Rye, came from Denmark, and the cameraman, all-important in a film exploiting photographic illusion, was Guido Seeber, while Wegener's wife, Lyda Salmanowa, played the leading woman's part. The story concerned the misfortunes of a student, Baldwin, who gives a Satanic sorcerer, Scapinelli (Paul Wegener), his image in the mirror in exchange for promises of wealth and marriage with a beautiful and aristocratic woman. The image in the mirror becomes Baldwin's evil self, and when he finally shoots it, he kills himself. The whole film is centred in Baldwin's undiscovered soul, the creation of a split personality. Wegener commissioned a special music score for the film, the first time this had happened in the German cinema. This remarkable production cost the producers, Deutsche Bioscop, a bare £1,000. Paul Wegener, both as actor and producer, was to become outstanding in the German cinema of the macabre after the war.

In addition to persuading established actors to make films, the cinema everywhere was to discover and develop its own players. In the case of Germany, the outstanding discovery of the period was Henny Porten,[8] who made her first appearance in 1907, the year of D. W. Griffith's introduction to the screen, in a brief projection of Elsa in *Lohengrin*. Her father, a member of Messter's staff, appeared in the title-role, and once again the gramophone produced the music. Henny Porten became the 'Messter girl', the as yet unnamed star of his company's films. In 1909 she was featured in *The Love of the Blind Girl* (*Das Liebesglück der Blinden*), a half-hour screenplay which she and her sister Rosa had scripted themselves, inspired by the familiar exterior of an Institute for the

Blind which they passed on their way to work. The pattern of events which followed was to be familiar alike in Germany and other countries—the public demanded to know who the pretty girl in the film really was. Messter gave way, and her name (like Mary Pickford's in the same year) appeared in all her future films. She then demanded a rise of 25s. in her monthly salary of £10, but this Messter at first refused. So she walked out of the studio. Messter, seeing she was serious, sent one of his assistants, Kurt Stark, to promise she should have the money. She returned, and later married Stark, her first husband, who was killed during the 1914–18 war.

Henny Porten was to become a favourite star; she was handsome, fair-haired and blue-eyed, a 'model' German girl. She was equally effective in comedy and drama. An entirely different kind of beauty was that of the mature, dark-haired Danish actress, Asta Nielsen [9] whose film, *The Abyss* (*Abgründe*, 1910), was a tragedy. It represented the ascendancy the Scandinavian cinema enjoyed in pre-war Germany, surpassing the public response to French, Italian or British films, and even those of the United States, though all these national industries had their agencies firmly established in Germany. Swedish and Danish films suited the German taste, and especially Asta Nielsen's strong, controlled miming in emotional parts, in which her large, expressive eyes and mobile face could be used to such effect. She had had years of experience on the stage before making films for Nordisk in Copenhagen. The producer and cinema-owner Paul Davidson,[10] head of Projektions A. G. Union, lost no time in bringing her to Germany, where she settled later with her husband and director, Urban Gad, after being offered a salary which was large for the period. She became a pin-up actress of the First World War, not only in Germany but in France as well. Her early biographer, Diaz, writing around 1920, quotes her on the importance of establishing physical detail for her characters, surrounding herself with appropriate objects as well as dressing in the right clothes. She accentuated her slenderness, and introduced strongly marked stripes into her costumes. She used gesture sparingly and without exaggeration, and moved her slim body with a passionate grace. She used facial expression with equal economy— a nod or a shake of the head with a smile, or a sudden flash of the

6

eye. She was one of the first actresses in the cinema to create a real, intense relationship with her characters. Paul Davidson, her producer, was a small, stocky man, very much on his dignity and wearing a monocle; he insisted on being called 'Herr General-direktor'.

By the time war was declared German film production was well established, with new studios near Berlin at Tempelhof and Neu-babelsberg.[11] But German production was small compared with the needs of her 2,000 cinemas, together with Austria's further 1,000. After August 1914 French, British and (later) American films could no longer appear on the screen. German production companies, numbering less than thirty in 1913, grew to some 250 by 1919 in order to supply the entertainment needs of a wartime public. The initial stepping up of German production reflected, as was natural, the nationalist type of film—representative titles have a familiar ring: *War Marriage, The Watch on the Rhine, The Call of the Fatherland, On the Field of Honour.* These were followed by a vast output of escapist films of little value. Among them, however, were certain films by a new young director, still in his early twenties, Ernst Lubitsch,[12] whose talents proved to be so considerable that some of the best artists in the German cinema of the period were in the end willing to work for him.

Lubitsch was born in 1892 in Berlin, and as a young man studied acting while working as a clerk in his father's clothing store. His teacher, one of Reinhardt's actors, introduced him into Reinhardt's company, where he played small supporting characters and appeared with many famous actors, including Paul Wegener, Alexander Moissi and Albert Bassermann. He took part in Reinhardt's production of *The Miracle* in 1912, which was filmed while the company was in England. From 1911, however, he was involved in films as a technical apprentice at Bioscop, and from 1913 he began to direct a series of short comedies. His first direction came with a subject he had scripted in a few minutes, and which Davidson accepted— *Miss Lather (Fräulein Seifenschaum),* in which Ossi Oswalda got her first starring part as a wartime girl barber who has to protect herself from the attentions of a customer by throwing the lather in his face—all done with an embryonic 'Lubitsch touch'! The first film in Lubitsch's comedy series was *Pinkus's Shoe Palace (Schuhpalast*

Pinkus, 1916); the series was to last until 1918, though at the same time Lubitsch continued to work in the theatre. His initial feature films, *The Eyes of the Mummy* (*Mumie Ma*) and *Carmen*, the first starring Emil Jannings [13] and both featuring Pola Negri,[14] were not made until the end of the war in 1918. Both were highly successful, and marked out Lubitsch as a director of spectacular dramatic subjects rather than the comedies which were nearer to his taste. Pola Negri persuaded him to become her director, and *The Eyes of the Mummy*, scripted by Hanns Kräly, was such a success that the far more ambitious film of *Carmen* was allocated to him. For this he used the chalk pits of Rüdersdorf, near Berlin, for the Spanish sierras, while a Spanish market square was erected in the studio grounds at Tempelhof. Both these films were made for UFA, the new production combine described later.

Other films of note made during the war period include Wegener's second film, *The Golem* (1915), part scripted and directed by Henryk Galeen,[15] a Dutchman working in Germany. Like *The Student of Prague*, *The Golem* was to be most effectively remade by Wegener and Galeen during the 1920s. The strange story of the Golem drew on the medieval Jewish legend which tells how a Rabbi infuses life into a statue of clay. The statue is excavated at a later period, and the secret which gives it life is discovered; it becomes a destructive monster when its love for a girl is frustrated. It 'dies' when it falls; lying shattered on the ground, it returns once more to clay. Wegener yet again explored a psychological, indeed a pathological, theme through fantasy. Another film dealing with a man-made monster at large was the serial, *Homunculus* (1916), in which an intelligent creature without a soul turns berserk, makes himself a dictator and takes his revenge on mankind. He has finally to be destroyed by a thunderbolt.

The most important event of the war years in the German cinema was the formation of Universum Film AG (UFA) in November 1917. General Ludendorff introduced an entirely new perspective for the cinema by recognizing its importance for propaganda and morale, and as a result creating under the German High Command a Photographic and Film Office (Bild und Film Amt, BUFA) to relate still and motion pictures to the war effort. Similar recognition on the industrial side led to the formation of the German

Cinematographic Company, for civilian and overseas propaganda; this was Deutsche Lichtbildgesellschaft (Deulig), backed by the financier Alfred Hugenberg and the press proprietor, Ludwig Klitzsch. This serious regard for the powers and importance of the cinema by the Army, by Government and by industry paved the way for the formation of the large 'umbrella' film organization, UFA, with capital of 25 million marks (£1,250,000), almost one third of which (8m. marks) was supplied by the Government, and the rest accumulated from various outside industrial sources by Georg Stauss of the Deutsche Bank. The leading film companies, such as Davidson's Projektions A. G. Union, Messter's company, German Nordisk, and the Austrian Sascha-Film, were affiliated to UFA, which acquired not only considerable production interests but a circuit of important cinemas. It had studios at Tempelhof, and a pre-release cinema in Berlin, the UFA Palace. With the companies, too, came their contract artists—from Davidson's company came Lubitsch and his script-writer, Hanns Kräly, Pola Negri and later Emil Jannings, as well as many others well known to German audiences. Vitascop brought UFA the services of Max Mack, while another affiliate brought in Asta Nielsen.

The one important company to remain at this stage outside the UFA combine was Deulig, which had Erich Pommer [16] as producer, since his own company, Decla, formed part of Deulig. The Austrian writer-director Fritz Lang [17] came to Germany to work for Deulig, having made his first film for Sascha-Film in Vienna, the company founded by the wealthy Alexander Count Kolowrat-Krokowsky, whom everyone called 'Sascha' and who had been a racing motorist in his youth. Sascha-Film brought many Austrian and Hungarian directors and actors into prominence, including Fritz Kortner,[18] Magda Sonja, Gustav Ucicky,[19] Mihály Kertész,[20] Josef Somlo and Alexander Korda.[21]

UFA, however, was to become the principal source for the many outstanding films produced in Germany during the great period of the 1920s. Although after the defeat of Germany in November 1918 the government stake in UFA was bought out, the company remained with its policy intact; in order to overcome the initial hostility abroad to everything German after the war, UFA acquired cinemas for itself in such countries as Spain, Holland, Switzerland

and in Scandinavia. At one stage or another virtually every great German actor or actress and every great director made films for this national corporation during the post-war years, which saw the rise and fall of the Weimar Republic and the final conquest of the state by Hitler in 1933.

Chapter two

The nineteen-twenties

The period 1919 to 1928, the year of the final establishment of the sound film, was one of great national upheaval in Germany. The country was defeated, but by no means destroyed; there was nothing of the cataclysmic destruction which faced Germany after the defeat of 1945. The first complications after the Armistice of November 1918 were political, between the right-wing nationalists and the left-wing social democrats. Geographically speaking Germany still represented a powerful nation situated between the entrenched capitalism of the Western Allies, with their new partner, the United States, and the unknown quantity of the Soviet Union, which was establishing itself as a Communist state. The sporadic attempts to create communist states in odd corners of Germany itself were abortive; the social democrats remained too firmly entrenched. The German armed forces permitted by the Allies for the nation's security were reduced to 100,000, and the notorious Free Corps movement, the self-appointed guardians of German bourgeois society against the intrusions of the left, grew up illegally.

After a period of economic instability which for a while turned Germany into a nation of beggars and gamblers and finally led to a catastrophic fall in the mark—wiping out large fortunes and small savings alike—the currency was stabilized in November 1923, and Germany entered on one of those phenomenal periods of hard work and rapidly growing prosperity of which she is so uniquely capable.[1] The Weimar Republic, so uncertain in its foundations during its earlier years, seemed to be establishing its authority in the face of such disruptive forces as the Communists and Fascists represented in the middle 1920s. Though Hitler's National Socialists managed to put twelve deputies into the Reichstag in 1928, no one could have forecast his landslide victories of the next five years. All through the middle nineteen-twenties there was a euphoric feeling that fresh industrial prosperity was within Germany's grasp, to which the United States was giving massive support by way of investment until the collapse of Wall Street in 1929.

In spite of social and economic difficulties the German film industry, led by UFA but by no means confined to it, was to achieve what came to be called a 'golden age' in quality of film-making. The huge number of films made—in 1921, for example, 246 features —rivalled that in the United States. Though the numbers were to drop as the length and overall quality of the films rose, in 1925, with 228 features, Germany had by far the largest output in Europe—in the same year, France produced 74 and Britain 44 films. In contrast with Hollywood, German film production, apart from UFA, was largely made up of independent producers who, on their very varying levels, gave individual attention to their products, while the United States was standardizing her films as the entertainments policies of the great corporations hardened under the dominant, showmen's personalities of the industry's leading producers. In addition to UFA, there were Decla and Bioscop, which amalgamated (with a capital of £1·5m.) in 1920, and then merged with UFA the following year, bringing Erich Pommer, Germany's outstanding producer, into association with UFA. Bioscop, it will be remembered, owned the great estate at Babelsberg, where the finest studios in Europe were to be constructed. Other companies included Terra, AAFA, Deulig, Süd-Film in Bavaria, Deutsche-Lichtspiel Syndikat (DLS), Phoebus and the Munich company of Emelka, founded by the celebrated Ostermayr brothers, Peter, Franz and Ottmar, who before the war had specialized in Bavarian scenic films going back to earlier years. Several of these companies, particularly among the latter as well as UFA, had considerable cinema interests and gave preferential treatment to their own product.[2]

The average, as distinct from the quality production of these and other smaller companies, provided the base from which many of the 'classics' of the German silent cinema arose. The spate of romantic historical films, with spectacular displays of costume and décor, which followed on the success of Lubitsch's *Madame Dubarry* (made in the early days of UFA in 1919), led to such outstanding films as Lang's *Nibelung Saga* (1924), while the mass-production of thrillers led to Lang's celebrated *Doctor Mabuse, the Gambler* (*Dr Mabuse, Der Spieler*, 1922) and *The Spy* (*Spione*, 1928). Films of legend and fantasy gave Arthur von Gerlach an opportunity to make his *Chronicle of the Grieshuus* (*Zur Chronik von Grieshuus*, 1925), and Ludwig Berger his delicate, poetic version of *Cinderella* (1923).

As we shall see, the abortive social upheavals manifest during the immediate post-war years in Germany found more permanent outlet in the arts than in politics. The popularization of pre-war expressionism, with its rather obvious psychological simplifications and symbolisms projected in painting and set design for the theatre, would inevitably penetrate the cinema, and did so for the first time in *From Morn to Midnight* (*Von Morgens bis Mitternacht*, 1919) directed by Karl Heinz Martin, and above all in *The Cabinet of Dr Caligari* (*Das Kabinett des Dr Caligari*, 1919); it was essentially a movement designed to get away from actuality and to satisfy the desire to probe seemingly fundamental truths of human nature and society by presenting them through fantasy and dramatized mysticism; of the expressionist films Carl Hauptmann, the eminent German novelist, claimed, 'The phenomena on the screen are the phenomena of the soul'. Expressionism was to exercise influences which declined into mere stylization of design rather than psychological manifestations of distraught 'souls' caught in the web of 'fate'. It became a generic term for many different forms of experiment and protest against convention, more especially in Germany. According to Lotte Eisner, writing in *Penguin Film Review* (No. 6, 1948):

The German intellectuals who would not and could not resign themselves to hard, plain reality, clung to their old reputation as a 'people of poets and thinkers', and endeavoured to take refuge in a sort of subconscious world full of anguish, unrest, and a vague remorse, obsessed by the memory of a glorious past. Everything became mysterious to those who had nothing to lose, and believed they possessed at least the treasures of mysticism; impenetrable mist seemed to cover the objects of a real world that had slipped out of their grasp.

This longing for chiaroscuro (as it were) found its ideal means of expression in film art. Here they were able to evolve in a visual but unreal manner phantoms created by their perturbed minds. In this unstable period, where all market values were soon to crash,

Germany seemed impregnated by an overwhelming sense of fatalism which was transformed into a violent art. The cruel gods of Valhalla, the ghosts of Eichendorff's romantic poetry, E. T. A. Hoffmann's demoniac fantasy, and Freud's psycho-analysis were all mixed together. They tortured themselves as they were soon going to torture others. They found a temporary escape in films formed in their own image, films of horror, death, and nightmare. This feeling gave a sort of glamour to the films of directors like Robert Wiene.

After every war or violent social upheaval which threatens the lives and security of large numbers of people, sexual impulses increase. The nineteenth century in authoritarian Germany, as elsewhere, had repressed sexual outlets, driving their expression underground in prostitution and pornography. Though it would be wrong to equate the morals of German society in the 1920s with the current 'permissiveness' in Europe and elsewhere, the 1920s were a period in which pre-war strictures in morality and social convention were thrown aside by the young, especially in Berlin. Girls shortened their hair and their skirts, and asserted their right to pre-marital sex. Berlin became the exhibitionist capital in Europe for clubs and other centres where voyeurism, homosexuality, transvestism and various sexual deviations were on display.

Germany, however, was not quite prepared for the outburst of sexuality in the immediate post-war cinema when for a while no form of censorship existed. Films which ostensibly dealt with sex education offered images of sexual indulgence to audiences both young and old—from sex hygiene to the sadder melodramas of prostitution and the exploitation of prurient curiosity about homosexuality and the like. Outstanding among the makers of this kind of film—which were known as *Aufklärungs Filme* (films of the facts of life)—was Richard Oswald, who made *Different from the Rest* (*Anders als die Andern*) about homosexuality and *Prostitution* during the period 1919–20. Producers at this time vied with one another to make quick money from these productions,[3] and the prevalence of sex on the screen led to the re-introduction of film censorship under the Reich Film Act of 29 May 1920. The Act was aimed deliberately at pornography and was not intended to be political; there was, in fact, a clause to this effect. Boards of censors operating in Berlin and Munich were empowered to examine every film intended for public exhibition, with the possibility of appeal against their decisions to a Supreme Censor Board. Children under twelve were excluded from the cinemas, and adolescents between twelve and eighteen were permitted to see only those films which received a certificate of suitability. The Reich Film Act also sought to protect native production from excessive competition from foreign imports by establishing the first quota regulation to occur in film history; the Act restricted foreign imports initially to 15 per cent of films projected in German cinemas, and amended this in January 1921 to a maximum of some 540,000 feet, or the equivalent of some ninety films of average length. The Act also imposed municipal entertainments tax on cinema seats, a regulation naturally opposed by the film industry in Germany, as elsewhere. There was, however, a distinction between the way Germany and other countries administered the tax: in Germany, exhibitors who showed films, both long and short, which were recognized by special committees representing cultural and educational interests as having artistic value enjoyed a reduction in taxes.

With production increasing on a considerable scale, film-makers turned everywhere for subjects, from contemporary best-sellers, such as Thea von Harbou's thrillers, to the heights of Thomas Mann—whose *Buddenbrooks* was adapted for the screen by Gerhard Lamprecht in 1928. The theatre provided what literature could not, including, for example, Pabst's fine adaptation of Wedekind's *Pandora's Box* (1929). The German taste for sentimental musicals and light opera was not frustrated, even during the silent film period; orchestras in the cinemas could be just as lively as those in the theatres while the action of the musicals and operettas was mimed on the screen. Films of the macabre were prominent not so much by their numbers as by their quality, but their fame and their psychological significance have been exaggerated out of all proportion in Siegfried Kracauer's brilliant but to some degree misleading book, *From Caligari to Hitler*. The forces which brought Hitler to power from comparative obscurity within a bare eight years after his release from confinement in Landsberg Castle were far nearer the ground than this. Equally macabre films were being made during this same period in 'gloomy' Sweden and in 'gay' France.[4]

The fashion for the macabre in German cinema was given its initial impetus by *The Cabinet of Dr Caligari*, a film which, owing to its fundamentally theatrical nature, represented a cul-de-sac in film technique. At this stage in film history it was, indeed, a complete and remarkable work of imaginative art which achieved an astonishing international reputation. This reputation grew during the 1920s as it was shown more widely abroad, and has given it a permanent place in film history. It was never widely shown in Germany.[5] It is by no means a perfect film, owing to certain disparities between the variety of talents who finally brought it together. The full account of the birth of the original story was revealed for the first time by Kracauer from information given him by one of the script-writers, the Czech poet Hans Janowitz. While in Hamburg in 1913 Janowitz believed himself to be the witness of the murder of a girl in a park near a fairground on the Reeperbahn, Hamburg's red-light area; later he attended the girl's funeral and believed that he saw her murderer there. The other author was the Austrian Carl Mayer,[6] whose wealthy father had turned him and his younger brother onto the street before committing suicide after gambling away his fortune. Mayer as an adolescent had undergone many painful psychiatric interviews when his mental condition was considered unstable. After the war, Janowitz had settled in Berlin and become a pacifist in violent reaction against authority; Mayer became his friend and shared his views. One night, in a fairground, they saw a strong man achieving his feats of strength apparently under hypnosis. From their combined experience the script was born, and they discovered the name Caligari in a volume of Stendhal's letters.

The story of the film—originally intended, according to Janowitz, to symbolize authority leading man into violence—showed how a succession of murders came to be committed in a small town in northern Germany. The murderer is a somnambulist, Cesare, played by Conrad Veidt,[7] clothed in skin-tight black and kept in a coffin-like cabinet; his actions are controlled by Caligari (Werner Krauss) [8] a crazy old showman and fortune-teller who tours the fairgrounds in a caravan and murders all those whose deaths his hypnotized victim foretells; one of those murdered is a young man, Alan, who with his friend, Francis, was in an audience in Caligari's fairground booth. Francis is determined to find his friend's murderer,

1 *Little Angel*
(*Engelein*), 1912.
Director, Urban Gad,
with Asta Nielsen.

2 *The Student of
Prague* (*Der Student
von Prag*), 1913.
Stellan Rye, with Paul
Wegener.

3 *Rose Bernd*, 1919.
Alfred Halms, with
Henny Porten.

4 *Veritas Vincit*, 1918.
Joe May, with Mia May.

5 *Passion* (*Madame Dubarry*), 1919. Ernst Lubitsch, with Pola Negri.

6 *Anna Boleyn*, 1920.
Ernst Lubitsch, with
Henny Porten and
Emil Jannings.

8, 9 *The Golem*, 1920.
Henryk Galeen, with
Paul Wegener.

7 *Hamlet*, 1920. Sven
Gade, with Asta
Nielsen.

10 *Sumurun*, 1920.
Ernst Lubitsch, with
Pola Negri.

11 *The Flame* (*Die
Flamme*), 1923. Ernst
Lubitsch, with Pola
Negri and Alfred Abel.

12 *From Morn to Midnight (Von Morgens bis Mitternacht)*, 1919. Karl Heinz Martin, with Roma Bahn and Ernst Deutsch.

13–16 *The Cabinet of Dr Caligari (Das Kabinett des Dr Caligari)*, 1919. Robert Wiene, with Werner Krauss and Conrad Veidt.

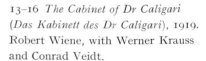

17 *Waxworks* (*Das Wachsfigurenkabinett*), 1924. Paul Leni, with Conrad Veidt.

18, 19 *Nosferatu*, 1922. F. W. Murnau, with Max Schreck.

20 *Vanina*, 1922. Arthur von Gerlach, with Asta Nielsen and Paul Wegener.

21 *The Hands of Orlac (Orlacs Hände)*, 1925. Robert Wiene, with Conrad Veidt.

22, 23 *The Student of Prague (Der Student von Prag)*, 1925. Henryk Galeen, with Paul Wegener and Conrad Veidt.

24, 25 *Destiny (Der Müde Tod)*, 1921. Fritz Lang, with Bernhard Goetzke and Lil Dagover.

26, 27 *Dr Mabuse, The Gambler (Dr Mabuse, der Spieler)*, 1922. Fritz Lang, with Rudolf Klein-Rogge and Alfred Abel.

28 *The Spy (Spione)*, 1928. Fritz Lang, with Rudolf Klein-Rogge.

29–32 *The Nibelung Saga (Die Nibelungen)*, 1924. Fritz Lang, with Paul Richter and Margarete Schön.

33–38 *Metropolis*, 1927. Fritz Lang, with Brigitte Helm, Alfred Abel, Gustav Fröhlich, Rudolf Klein-Rogge.

39 *The Woman in the Moon* (*Die Frau im Mond*), 1928. Fritz Lang, with Willy Fritsch and Gerda Maurus.

40 *Faust*, 1926. F. W. Murnau, with Emil Jannings and Gösta Ekman.

41, 42 *Tartuffe*, 1925. F. W. Murnau, with Emil Jannings, Lil Dagover and Werner Krauss.

43 *Fridericus Rex*, 1923. Arzen von Czerépy, with Otto Gebühr.

44 *Manon Lescaut*, 1927. Arthur Robison, with Lya de Putti and Vladimir Gaiderov.

45 *Cinderella (Der Verlorene Schuh)*, 1923. Ludwig Berger, with Helga Thomas and Paul Hartmann.

46 *Hedda Gabler*, 1924. Sven Gade, with Asta Nielsen and Albert Steinrück.

47–50 *The Last Laugh (Der Letzte Mann)*, 1925. F. W. Murnau, with Emil Jannings.

51 *The Street* (*Die Strasse*), 1923. Karl Grune, with Eugen Kloepfer and Aud Egede Nissen.

52 *Shattered* (*Scherben*), 1921. Lupu Pick, with Werner Krauss and Edith Posca.

53, 54 *Madame Does Not Want Children* (*Madame wünscht keine Kinder*), 1925. Alexander Korda, with Maria Corda and Harry Liedtke.

55, 56 *Nju*, 1924.
Paul Czinner, with
Elisabeth Bergner.

57 *Vaudeville* (*Variété*),
1925. Ewald André
Dupont, with Emil
Jannings.

58–60 *Secrets of a Soul*
(*Geheimnisse einer
Seele*), 1926. G. W.
Pabst, with Emil
Jannings.

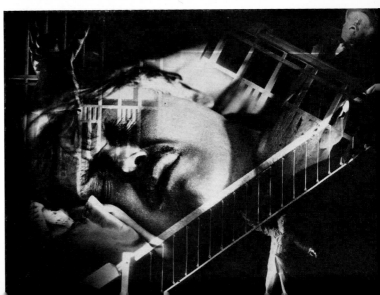

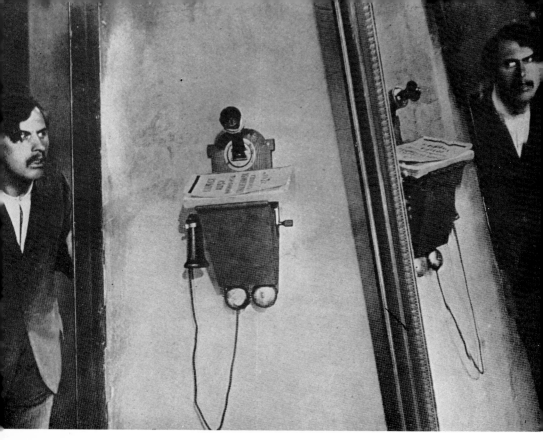

61, 62 *The Love of Jeanne Ney* (*Die Liebe der Jeanne Ney*), 1927. G. W. Pabst, with Wladimir Sokoloff, Brigitte Helm, Jack Trevor.

63 *The Joyless Street* (*Die Freudlose Gasse*), 1925. G. W. Pabst, with Asta Nielsen and Greta Garbo.

64, 65 *Pandora's Box* (*Die Büchse der Pandora*), 1929. G. W. Pabst, with Louise Brooks.

66 *Berlin, Symphony of a Great City* (*Berlin, Die Symphonie einer Grosstadt*), 1927. Karl Freund, with Carl Mayer and Walter Ruttmann.

67 *Accident* (*Überfall*), 1929. Ernö Metzner.

68 *The Adventures of Prince Achmed* (*Die Geschichte des Prinzen Achmed*), 1926. Lotte Reiniger.

69 *Ways to Strength and Beauty* (*Wege zur Kraft und Schönheit*), 1925. Nicolas Kaufmann.

and after many adventures he finally associates what has happened with Cesare, and through him, with Caligari. He pursues the old man to a lunatic asylum. Here, to his horror, he finds that Caligari is the psychiatric director. Faced with the corpse of Cesare, the authoritarian director collapses into raving madness. Reason, in the person of Francis, has overcome murderous, authoritarian unreason, in the person of Caligari.

Pommer, as producer, had tried to sign Fritz Lang to direct the film, but he was already committed to another. Pommer therefore gave the production to Robert Wiene; [9] it happened that Wiene's father, an actor, had become mentally unstable in his old age. But under the influence of both Lang and Wiene, who saw the story merely as a good plot for a melodrama, the beginning and end were changed in such a way as to lose entirely the political and psychological implications intended by Janowitz and Mayer. The plot was inset in another story, which showed the whole action to be a figment in Francis's mind. He is mad, and Caligari, an utterly benevolent man who closes the film, sane! It is Francis who ends up in a strait-jacket. No amount of protest by the authors convinced Pommer, Meinert, Pommer's associate producer, or Wiene that the new version was not superior as *entertainment* to the original.

But, if the political significance was wholly lost, certain psychological and expressionist elements were very fully developed, giving the film an atmosphere of extraordinary, compelling, even hypnotic power and visual beauty. The designer Janowitz had wanted was Alfred Kubin, an early surrealist painter; this was overruled by Pommer and his associates, and the sets, designed to be cheaply produced, were devised in the expressionist manner by Hermann Warm, Walter Röhrig and Walter Reimann, [10] who all belonged to the Berlin Sturm group; convinced expressionists, they believed (in Warm's words) that 'films must be drawings brought to life'. The result was the extraordinary curves and whorls painted on screens, the rostra set at strident angles, the figurative alleyways, houses, roofs, walls and balustrades, all set in curiously stylized relations to each other. Imaginatively lit and photographed by Willie Hameister, these sets gave the film, together with the magnificently stylized, concentrated performances by Veidt and Krauss, its lasting fascination. The film was originally tinted in blue and amber. On occasion even titling was incorporated into this madman's universe—'*Ich muss Caligari werden*', and so forth, spelt out in jerkily animated letters across the sky. Apart from its startling design and dramatic atmosphere, the film used few technical innovations, and no dynamic cutting. The camera remained static, like a spectator in the theatre. There was, however, an intelligent use of the iris-in and -out for significant punctuation of the slowly evolving narrative, presented by a succession of long-held shots, each one of which was as beautifully composed and lit as it was strikingly designed. One anomaly has been frequently pointed out; the expressionist sets remain when the action returns to mental normality. It is as if the original authors achieved a subtle revenge for the misrepresentation of their purpose. It was to be Janowitz's only film; for Carl Mayer it was to be the beginning of a notable career as a screen-writer.

The actual influence of *The Cabinet of Dr Caligari*, even in Germany, remained comparatively small, in spite of its widespread reputation. Surrealism, as Janowitz and Mayer had hinted, and not expressionism, was to become the organic link of the cinema to the non-rational and the subconscious; expressionism belonged rather to the painter and, by application, to theatrical décor in the 1920s. As the film advanced into its own creative domain, it left expressionism behind and took to the newer, far more permanent and fundamental influences of surrealism. But meanwhile the *réclame* of this film among the intellectuals meant that, in spite of its shortcomings, it could not go uncopied. Among the films it directly influenced were the Russian Martian fantasy, *Aelita* (made by Alexandra Exter of the Moscow Kamerny Theatre) and the re-make of *The Student of Prague*. Wiene himself re-used the technique with little success in *Genuine* (1920), the story of an oriental priestess who destroys the men she enslaves; this was scripted by Carl Mayer. Expressionism as such must be distinguished from the visual projection of the macabre or of legendary magic and fantasy in which the stylization exists solely to create dramatic atmosphere, not a state of the 'soul'. Stylization in sets and photographic illusion was to become an important part of German studio presentation during the 1920s, of much wider application than strict expressionism. After *Genuine* Wiene went on to make *The Hands of Orlac* (*Orlacs*

18

Hände, 1925, with Conrad Veidt and Fritz Kortner), an essay in Grand Guignol which depended entirely on the intensity of Veidt's performance as a pianist obsessed by the idea that he has been given the hands of an assassin after a railway accident, and that as a result his whole character is changing.[11]

The dedication of the German film to the studio, and to the exact plastic control which the artificial combination of décor, lighting and photographic techniques could achieve, was shown in the great spectacular films for which UFA was to be principally responsible from 1919. Among the first of these were Joe May's *Veritas Vincit* (1918), with Mia May, static lions and agitated crowds, and Ernst Lubitsch's series—*Madame Dubarry* (sometimes titled *Passion*, 1919, with Pola Negri and Emil Jannings), *Anna Boleyn* (1920, with Henny Porten and Jannings), Reinhardt's *Sumurun* (sometimes titled *One Arabian Night*, 1920, with Pola Negri), and *The Loves of Pharaoh* (*Das Weib des Pharao*, 1921, with Emil Jannings), all scripted by Hanns Kräly. *The Loves of Pharaoh* was one of the most spectacular films of the era. It has been described by Theodore Huff:

The Loves of Pharaoh was one of the most spectacular pictures ever produced, belonging in the same epic class with *Cabiria*, *Intolerance*, *Theodora*, *The Thief of Bagdad* and *Ben Hur*. Although the picture cost only about $75,000, it would have cost a million or more in the U.S.A.: ancient Egypt was reconstructed on a large scale and peopled with thousands. The magnificent sets and tremendous crowd scenes were overwhelming. It was further distinguished by Jannings' portrait of the powerful and cruel, yet pathetic and human Pharaoh, whose inability to win love causes his downfall. The picture, never having been revived, is not well known today, but it is one of Jannings' greatest roles. If the earlier German and Lubitsch pictures were inferior to American pictures photographically, by 1921 they had an opportunity to study the latest American films, and equalled them in technique. (In two or three years *The Last Laugh* and *Variety* were to surpass American photographic technique.) The lighting in *The Loves of Pharaoh* was exceptional and dramatic. For instance, in the great throne room, the foreground crowd was left in shadow, the pillars lit in such a way that the eye was drawn to the distant throne action, etc. The continuity was also much improved and smoother with use of the American technique of parallel action and other cinematic devices.

All this was grafted onto Lubitsch's unique genius for mass effects and humanly dramatic personal scenes. The triangle story of king, favorite, and former young lover was becoming a little familiar in German films by now. In this case the picture was a mixture of spectacle and psychological drama as the mind of the Pharaoh was studied and revealed.

Lubitsch told Heinrich Fraenkel later in Hollywood that he had been much influenced in his decorative deployment of crowd scenes in these films by Mauritz Stiller's Swedish production, *Herr Arne's Treasure* (1919), but that it was his later film, *Erotikon* (1920) which guided his interest towards the intimate films, the *Kammerspiel* (that is, intimate drama), in which he later came to specialize. He left for Hollywood in 1922, where he made the following year *The Marriage Circle*, *Three Women*, and *Forbidden Paradise*.

Lubitsch's most typical work was to be created outside Germany; when he left for the United States he was still under thirty. But his highly successful career in Germany gave him great experience in the techniques of film-making. *Madame Dubarry*, the story of Louis XV and his mistress, was more than mere spectacle; Lubitsch concentrated on his actors, insisting that they gave some semblance of reality to their performances. He was called in consequence by some critics the 'humanizer of history', used as they were to the marionette-like characterization more typical of the period. The film had reached the screen at the time of the collapse of the German monarchy. Lubitsch's detailed attention to acting, as well as his humour, is seen in his German films made on a smaller scale, the comedies *The Oyster Princess* (*Die Austernprinzessin*, 1919) with Ossi Oswalda, a satire on the American businessman, *The Doll* (*Die Puppe*, 1919), also with Ossi Oswalda, a highly stylized fantasy of a doll coming to life using expressionist sets combined with elements of farce and light opera, *Kohlhiesel's Daughters* (*Kohlhiesel's Töchter*, 1920), with Henny Porten and Emil Jannings, a peasant comedy, and *The Wild Cat* (*Die Bergkatze*, 1921) with Pola Negri, in which he set an expressionist castle, designed by Ernst Stern from Reinhardt's theatre, in a real Alpine location—all these films in one way or another pointed ahead to his work in America. His final film in Germany, *The Flame* (*Die Flamme*, sometimes re-titled *Montmartre*, 1923, with Pola Negri) was set in the Paris of 1860 and concerned a *demi-mondaine* trying to redeem herself; by this time he had already been invited to go to the United States and direct Mary Pickford in *Rosita*. Hanns Kräly, who had worked on the scripts of all these films as well as on the spectacles, went to Hollywood with him.

The 'Lubitsch touch', important at this stage in the cinema because of its insistence on the small, revealing detail of action, has been defined as a swift innuendo or rapier-like comment accomplished by a brief shot of telling action, conveying far more than words in a moment of time. Typical is this scene in *The Flame*, played by Pola Negri: a wife, wondering whether or not she should leave her husband, sits alone in her boudoir, seated at her dressing-table. Concentrating on her hands, which move nervously, we see her fingering her wedding-ring, twisting it, then taking it off, weighing it in the palm of her hand. Slowly, she puts it in a drawer of her dressing-table, but in front, in easy reach. She takes an empty box, puts the ring in it, and thrusts the box back in the drawer. The sudden violence of this action overturns the silver-framed photograph of her husband. This frightens her; she sits rigid in a moment of panic. The action then goes into reverse. She sets the photograph upright; she takes the ring from its box, almost playfully; smiling, she puts the ring back on her finger, jumps up, and runs from the room into her husband's arms. Told in words, this is tedious. In half a minute of action on the screen, its detail and symbolism combine to make, for its period, a revelation of what the film could achieve in the hands of an inventive film-maker. Moreover, it was visual, and this stood Lubitsch in good stead when he left Germany; he was never to learn to speak English fluently, and his pronunciation of it was always atrocious.

While Lubitsch was lured away to Hollywood, Fritz Lang remained in Germany until Hitler's rise to power drove him out. His principal films span the 1920s in a great arc of achievement: *Destiny* (*Der Müde Tod—The Weary Death*—1921, with Lil Dagover and Bernhard Goetzke), *Dr Mabuse, the Gambler* (*Dr Mabuse, Der Spieler*, 1922, in two parts, with Rudolf Klein-Rogge), *The Nibelung Saga* (*Die Nibelungen*, 1924, in two parts, *Siegfried's Death* and *Kriemhild's Revenge*, with Paul Richter and Margarete Schön), *Metropolis* (1927, with Alfred Abel, Gustav Fröhlich, Rudolf Klein-

Rogge, Brigitte Helm), *The Spy* (*Spione*, 1928, with Rudolf Klein-Rogge), and *The Woman in the Moon* (*Die Frau im Mond*, 1928, with Willy Fritsch and Gerda Maurus).

In an article written for *Penguin Film Review* in 1948, Lang described the atmosphere in which he worked during the early 1920s:

The First World War brought changes to the Western world. In Europe, an entire generation of intellectuals embraced despair. In America too, intellectuals and artists turned to a rocky wasteland, trying to outdo each other in pessimistic outcry. All over the world, young people engaged in the cultural fields, myself among them, made a fetish of tragedy, expressing open rebellion against the old answers and outworn forms, swinging from naive nineteenth-century sweetness and light to the opposite extreme of pessimism for its own sake. In the end, our audience, even in Europe where a new life was being built out of the wreckage of the old, rejected our despair (at the box-office!) and we, with many groans, gave in to the 'bad taste' of the audience while casting wistful glances back into the purple gloom in which our 'artistic' spirits had thrived. Yes, it was a fight I shared, the fight for the 'unhappy ending,' but to-day I believe I was tilting with windmills.

Looking at those old films again for the first time since he had left Germany, he has been quoted by David Robinson as saying that he was upset at finding the moral of *Metropolis* so facile ('Labour and Capital—Hand and Brain united by the Heart'), but not displeased with his forecast of the future ('in 1924 I am already prophesying overhead motorways'). Robinson continues:

Apart from the Nibelungs, all Lang's silent films share a novelette quality which they most likely owe to the contribution of Thea von Harbou, then Lang's wife and—from *The Spiders* to *The Testament of Dr Mabuse*—his constant scenarist. Still, it is possible confidently to attribute the choice of the themes to Lang himself. The German cinema of that period was strangely under the spell of tyrants and monsters; but it was Lang who brought to apotheosis the romantic, anarchic master-criminal. The same motif appears in practically all his films, *The Spiders*, *Mabuse*, *The Spy* and, more marginally, *Metropolis* and *The Woman in the Moon* are all concerned with the destructive machinations of power-crazed criminals, inciting or hypnotizing others into doing their nefarious work.

Thea von Harbou [12] stayed behind in Nazi Germany, and the senti-mental, melodramatic themes dropped out of his films; he went on to make such uncompromising American masterpieces as *Fury* (1936) and *You Only Live Once* (1937) in the United States.

We do not look at Fritz Lang's silent films, therefore, for any profound social meaning. Kracauer, as one would expect, views them as symptoms of Germany's *malaise*; influenced by Spengler's *The Decline of the West*, artists turned to stories which foreshadowed the inevitable doom of civilized man, overcome either by magically-endowed tyrants or the upheavals of anarchy. *Destiny*, which only enjoyed a *succès d'estime* in Germany after its success abroad as a 'typically Germanic' work, is a legend-like fable in which Death, or Fate, takes possession of a young girl and her lover; when she challenges him in a dream to spare their lives she passes through a series of experiences in the past in which her attempts to save her life and that of her lover fail. The film ends with her own voluntary death in order to share Elysium with her dead lover. Destiny, Kracauer claims, becomes one with victorious tyranny, even though Death, a sympathetic figure, would have it otherwise. Man cannot win once Fate is against him. The film remains one of Lang's most brilliant cinematic achievements. The designers were the same as for *Caligari*, Warm and Röhrig; Lang kept the fantasy of the sets under a firm, architectural control.

Dr Mabuse, the Gambler was a very different film, a thriller in two parts which Lang was to claim as a 'documentary' or 'docu-ment' reflecting the current world situation. Mabuse, whose identity is concealed behind a miscellany of disguises, uses hypnosis to control his victims and opponents. He is finally overcome, and is discovered to be mad. He inhabits an anarchic, amoral and expres-sionist world of stylized sets; Kracauer sees in him a symbol of crazed, anti-social power, uniting tyranny with chaos; from Lang's point of view at the time the film was just a good box-office thriller.

Dr Mabuse was succeeded by yet another style of film—the two-part *Nibelung Saga—Siegfried's Death* and *Kriemhild's Revenge*. This was intended to be a projection of Germanic culture as well as a great pictorial epic; it weaves together the traditional stories in such a way as to emphasize, in Thea von Harbou's words, 'the inexorability with which the first guilt entails the last atonement'.

In the first part Siegfried conquers the dragon and wins Kriemhild, sister of the weakling Gunther, King of the Burgundians, as his wife by using his magic powers to overcome Brunhild, an Amazonian princess. When Brunhild discovers how she was conquered, she has Siegfried slain. Kriemhild achieves her revenge in the second part by marrying Attila, King of the Huns, and with his aid, slaughtering the Burgundians while at the same time causing her own death. Her dream in *Siegfried's Death*, a study in abstract cinema, was made for Lang by Walter Ruttmann. The whole legendary story becomes an inexorable display of passion, hatred and violence. Lang brings a vast, solid pictorialism to the film; the world of make-believe has a decorative, structural actuality alike in its palaces and cathedrals, its woodlands and forests, its underground caverns inhabited by dwarfs. The dragon in *Siegfried's Death* remains one of the best-realized of screen monsters, controlled by a team of operators stationed both inside and beneath the monster, which was some twenty metres long. In spite of its lavish treatment, the film gives the overall impression of austerity of design, and of an absolute symmetry. Every movement is slow and stately, but always when possible the film emphasizes the violence implicit in the story. Writing after seeing the film many times during the decade following its initial release, Roger Manvell said:

Siegfried and his warrior kings observe strict formation in the Burgundian court, and processions and church services alike are seen to be perfect in their pictorial symmetry. If this exact symmetry oppresses you, then the architecture of *Siegfried* with its vast, spacious walls, its balance of curved masses with angular masses, its geometrically patterned floors and its long flights of steps will soon become a visual bore. But if you like symmetry, then you will find (for a time, at least) a nobility and grandeur in these palaces and courts, and in the costumes with their equally symmetrical designs from the Reinhardt theatre.

The most impressive and beautiful scenes in the film are those in the forests, the misty glades and the caverns through which Siegfried has to travel before he reaches the Kingdom of Burgundy. After many viewings spread over nearly twenty years I still find the sequence of Siegfried's approach to the dragon through the tall trees one of the most beautiful in the silent cinema, and the dragon himself (controlled by a team of men inside his framework) the most impressive of all the screen's giant monsters. The descent into the cave holding the Rhine treasure hoard is a wonderful studio spectacle, and the shot of the slowly petrifying dwarfs is completely convincing. One's memory of this long film returns in the end to these scenes, or to those of the ride of Siegfried on his horse led by Alberic through the mists, and his death at the end of the film in the little artificial glade.

The rest of the film is best projected at sound speed. This substantially quickens the intolerably slow pace of the action in the midst of architectural sets which appear increasingly cold and dead as the film develops.

With *Metropolis* Lang concentrated his pictorialism upon the future. It was his first sight of New York from the Atlantic which had given him the visual idea for this project; the ingenuity of German camera-work, in particular the celebrated Schüftan process which, by the use of mirrors, could combine sets which were life-size in the acting area and miniatures above. This was necessary for a film which not only projected large-scale vistas of a luxurious city of skyscrapers above ground, with their overhead roads, but a vast underground city housing the slave-workers and the Moloch-like factories which devoured their labour. In addition, there were symbolic fantasy sets—the dream image of Moloch itself into whose devouring body the processions of automata-workers march, the tower of Babel, and the robot image of Maria, the saintly leader of the workers, manufactured in the strange laboratory of the mad inventor, Rotwang, the tool of the dictator, in order that her evil image may supplant that of the saint. The dictator's sympathetic son descends to help the workers, and falls in love with the true Maria; through his intervention the naive conclusion is reached in which the workers' representative shakes hands with the dictator, symbolizing thereby the union of brain and labour through the supremacy of the heart. Naturally, *Metropolis* was to become one of Hitler's favourite films, with its illusion of the ultimate benevolence of the master-race.[13] H. G. Wells when he saw the film regarded it as ludicrous and sentimental.

With *The Spy*, another brilliantly made thriller, Lang conceived a story which is not about spying as such, but the power struggle of rival gangs in an anarchic world, in which the master-spy, like Mabuse, sinks his own identity under a succession of disguises. Kracauer dismisses this film, and for that matter *The Woman in the Moon*, as mere studio nonsense. However, Paul Rotha wrote of the latter contemporaneously:

The elaborate staging of the rocket's departure, the surging of the crowds at the hangar, the scenes inside the projectile during the journey, the extraordinary glare of the lunar landscape, these are achieved with a conviction and reality that are possible only in a German film studio. All the intricate mechanical apparatus in the rocket, for example, is magnificently solid and real. Wheels, dials, twisted pipes, cylinders, steel ladders, and a hundred other details are obviously the result of clever craftsmanship. They may be impossible but they have the appearance of reality, and that is what matters. The surface of the moon, covered with a white powdered dust against a background of distant rocky mountains, is an amazing feat of studio construction. So also are the queer bubbling pools of oily liquid and the great lumps of gold in the twisted clefts of the rocks. I know of no other artists who can stage such things with so great a degree of sincerity and rightness as the Germans.

Rotha criticizes, however, the lack of dynamic film sense in the editing, as distinct from the handling of the individual shots.

Lotte Eisner, the friend and latter-day interpreter of Lang, has emphasized the important part surface, mass and light play in the visual composition of his work, not only in his German films but in his later American productions. She shows how he borrowed only fractionally from expressionist design, and was motivated by other, far wider considerations:

Before Wiene shot *The Cabinet of Dr Caligari* the subject was offered to Fritz Lang. It is useless to conjecture how this film would have turned out under his direction. When two years later he shot *Destiny*, it was, like *Caligari*, a film of expressionist atmosphere. But while the fantastically distorted settings of *Caligari* resulted in an intentionally flat and linear picture, Lang's architectural sense overcame the more purely graphic style of the original expressionists. His small medieval town somewhere in Germany is, in spite of its fantasy, more real than the one the somnambulist Cesare haunts owing to the subtle use of light which creates a sense of architectural depth.

A German critic once pointed out the preponderant part light plays in the *mise en scène* of his countrymen; he called this method 'light as a dramatic factor'. German directors liked to use spotlights placed lower than the settings to be lit in order to create curiously unreal contrasts and extraordinary shadows; they accentuate angles in order to exaggerate their sharp outlines. For Lang, however, light is a means of emphasising the form and structure of his settings. Yet the basic idea of light as a means of obtaining dramatic effect is at its best in *Metropolis*, when the mad inventor's torch chases Maria until she is caught in a circle of light out of which there seems to be no escape. (The intermittent light of an electric advertisement-sign obsessing the sick brain of the cashier-murderer in *Scarlet Street* has a similar effect.)

Light also helps Lang to create atmosphere in an almost impressionist manner; through luminous, transparent reflections he creates a kind of counterpoint between the lighting and the settings. Sometimes he chooses natural sources of lighting; in *Liliom*, for instance, he tried on the set for more than one hour to capture the vision of flickering lights from a turning merry-go-round reflected on a greyish wall. For the search in the brushwood in *M* enormous spotlights were pointed on to shrubs which had previously been sprinkled with water in order to show a kaleidoscope of gleaming drops.[14]

Expressionism, in one form or another, found its final outlet alike in the thriller and the films of fantasy and the macabre, for which Germany won a reputation during the earlier 1920s quite disproportionate to her actual output of such work. Virtually all these films were confined to the period up to 1925, when the higher levels of the German film began to move closer to realism and darker psychological subjects, particularly in the work of G. W. Pabst. Wiene, as we have seen, followed up his relative success in *Caligari* with *Genuine*, using expressionist sets; this, too, had been scripted by Mayer. Genuine is the name of an Oriental priestess who is sold as a slave to an old man who confines her in a glass cage until she lures a young man to kill him. She then indulges in excesses with every man she can seduce. The sets were by Cesar Klein, but both décor and actors failed to create the same integrated world of the macabre which makes *Caligari* so singularly effective. Wiene, not to be defeated, made one more attempt at full expressionism in his adaptation of *Crime and Punishment* called *Raskolnikov* (1923, with Grigory Chmara); the sets were designed by the architect, Andrei Andreiev. This film was more successful and managed to create an environment to which the acting could respond and which reflected the hallucinations of despair possessing the student's mind, as in the notable sequences of the Coroner embedded in a spider's web and of Raskolnikov's dream. The cast for this film came from the Moscow Arts Theatre. It was sponsored by one of Germany's most enterprising producers, Hanns Neumann, who was to make, among many other films, the first film on Frederick the Great, *Sturm und Drang* (see below, page 33), the film of the life of Christ, *I.N.R.I.*, and Pabst's psychological film *Secrets of a Soul.*

Another 'expressionist' film was *Vanina* (1922, directed by Arthur von Gerlach, with Asta Nielsen and Paul Wegener); it was adapted from Stendhal by Mayer. The story concerns the daughter of a crippled and sadistic tyrant ruler whose subjects rebel, led by a young man, Octavio, with whom Vanina is in love. The rebellion is crushed, but the tyrant delights in seeming to permit his daughter to marry Octavio only to have him seized during the wedding ceremony and condemned to be hanged. Although Vanina extorts a pardon from her father and tries to get away from his clutches with her lover, Octavio is finally murdered and Vanina dies of a broken heart. Perhaps the most celebrated sequence in this film was the one which prolongs the agony of the lovers' attempted flight by making it a study in suspense—Vanina and Octavio pass in slow motion down an endless succession of corridors which symbolize the ultimate impossibility of escape. They are sustained only by a hope which proves to be false.

The macabre took on as many forms as familiar legends of the supernatural could offer the expertise of the designers, studio technicians and the cinematographers. Wegener and Galeen repeated *The Golem* (1920), though they gave their second version a different slant and employed the German architect Hans Poelzig, who had worked for Reinhardt, to design their Gothic sets for the medieval ghetto. Wegener plays the Monster, created by the Rabbi Loew, which is finally overcome through the innocence of a child. This version also includes the terrorization of the Emperor who is prevented from expelling the Jews from their ghetto by the vision of Ahasuerus conjured up by the Rabbi to threaten the destruction of the Imperial Palace. Only after this projection of wishful thinking, which is nevertheless in the context of the story very effective, does the Rabbi create the Golem. The 1915 version of the film, it will be remembered, takes place long after the Rabbi's death, when the Golem is excavated and comes to life for the second time.

In 1922 came *Warning Shadows* (*Schatten*, with Fritz Kortner and Fritz Rasp), Arthur Robison's remarkable film projecting the subconscious hallucinations of six people, the jealous husband, the amorous wife, and her four potential lovers. Visions of what might happen should they finally succumb to their various passions are prompted by a travelling showman, creator of shadow plays which develop into projections of the future when he puts his subjects into an hypnotic trance. The violent nightmares enacted by the shadows bring about a collective cure; the hypnotist acts as the equivalent of a psychiatrist purging the poison from the subconscious minds of the dreamers. The situation may seem melodramatic and absurd, but the visual presentation of the film, with its chiaroscuro photography and the heightened, trance-like mime of the actors, creates a silent ballet, a symbolic pantomime, interspersed by the 'warning shadows', silhouettes projected on the screen, or onto the translucent shades of windows lit from behind, like independent, menacing forces. Robison introduces images reflected in mirrors, which themselves betray those whom they reflect.

In *Waxworks* (*Das Wachsfigurenkabinett*, 1924)—with Wilhelm Dieterle,[15] Jannings, Veidt and Krauss—Paul Leni,[16] working with Galeen as his script-writer, made a three-part film developed from the waxwork figures in a fair—Harun-al-Raschid (Jannings), Ivan the Terrible (Veidt), and Jack the Ripper (Krauss). Again, this film is highly stylized; Leni had been one of Reinhardt's set designers, and consequently looked on the film from the designer's point of view. A young poet (Dieterle) is hired by a showman to create stories for his wax figures of these three pathological sadists —the first becomes a mere burlesque, but the study of Ivan takes sadism to a fine point as his poisoned victims are left to forecast the moment of their deaths in the Emperor's giant hour-glass. Finally he himself is driven mad when subjected to a fate similar to that of his victims. In the final, framing episode the poet and the showman's daughter are also involved in a nightmare experience, during which they are chased through the deserted fairground by the ultimate murderer in the popular imagination, Jack the Ripper. As Lotte Eisner points out, the expressionism in the design of

Waxworks is more decorative than symbolic, and is varied considerably to meet the different atmospheres of each episode, the last being closest to *Caligari* in design and feeling, while that of Ivan is largely design achieved by placing decoratively costumed figures in areas of light and shadow. There is a moment when Ivan stands in a folding door as if he were a painted figure forming part of an icon.

In 1925 came the new version of *The Student of Prague* (with Conrad Veidt), which Galeen directed. Veidt gave a magnificent performance as the student struggling with himself to the point of death. A study of this film published in *Close-Up* (September 1927), shortly after its first screening, gives a woman's reaction:

The Student of Prague, the famous fencer Baldwin is cut by fencing companies, societies. What you will. He is thrown into the arms of the common Alma Tademesque little violet seller. Things march from worse to still worse. This is what comes of selling one's shadow to a stranger. There is, as is obvious, the really clever stalking of the shadow and the merging and cross-currents of two images. We never lose sight of the identity of either; this too is a triumph. The spectre is the slim gaunt creature in the early student get-up, the man is the somewhat out at heels distrait discarded gentleman. The spectre grows in distinction, in power apparently. The man diminishes. The spectre remains the Student of Prague and Baldwin, his begetter is hounded by his Frankenstein. Doors are no impediment. The spectre in triumph of film-photography glides discreetly through and into the most sacred milieu. Baldwin the man sinks into the scum of fetid cellars. The spectre and the little early mistress, the small common, yet uncommonly pretty, violet-girl sink with him. Baldwin becomes violent, destructive. The spectre shares his evil end, gloats in it. Yet apart . . . having some life outside humanity . . . following, following, till we want to scream, 'strangle him, get rid of him, one or the other, let this duality perish if Baldwin perish with it.'

Baldwin does so finally perish, having lured the shadow back into the frame of the mirror in the now deserted attic. He shoots the spectre only to find himself bleeding with the bullet wound. The bullet aimed so adroitly at the breast of the image in the mirror has, by some psychic affinity, entered his own heart. So dies Baldwin.

In these films, and others which belong to the height of studio achievement in Germany, much obviously depended on the photography. Two of the leading camera directors of the 1920s were Fritz Arno Wagner (1889 – 1950), who lit among other films *Nosferatu, Warning Shadows, The Chronicle of the Grieshuus, The Love of Jeanne Ney, The Spy* and *The Woman in the Moon*, to mention silent films only, and Karl Freund (1890 – 1969) who, before he went to Hollywood in 1929, shot *The Golem* of 1920, *Lucrezia Borgia, The Last Laugh, Tartuffe, Metropolis, Vaudeville, Faust*, as well as Ruttmann's documentary, *Berlin, Symphony of a Great City*. If photography can be defined as painting a scene with light, this is what these artist-photographers achieved, using selected points of highlight framed with shadows, building compositions of light and shade, flooding the image with mist, dissolving it with super-impositions, giving it magic by means of multiple exposures, and creating vast perspectives with illusory height and depth through the Schüftan and other processes for marrying sections of models to sections of life-size sets. Theirs was the technical skill and artistry which realized in terms of two-dimensional images in black-and-white, shadow and light, mist and illumination the imaginary visions of directors as different as Lang and Pabst, Wiene and Murnau, and the men who designed and built their sets.

F. W. Murnau's *Nosferatu* (*Nosferatu, Eine Symphonie des Grauens*, literally, 'Nosferatu, a Symphony of Terror', 1922), with Max Schreck, was adapted by Henryk Galeen from Bram Stoker's famous story of vampirism, *Dracula*.[17] Nosferatu is the vampire, lying by day in a sarcophagus he keeps in his forest castle; at night he goes out to prey on the civilized world, bringing pestilence wherever he appears until he is challenged by the positive forces of good embodied in a girl who refuses to be afraid of him and so destroys him. Some credit for the achievement in this early work by Murnau, one of the masters in German cinema, should go to Wagner for his highly creative camera-work; he obtained wonderfully luminous images in the ghostly woodlands surrounding the castle (seen in negative), in the phosphorescent water through which a ship filled with the dead moves silent and untended, in his close-ups of omnivorous plants, and the procession of coffins seen from above moving down the streets of Bremen. The whole of nature is seen to be disturbed by the presence of evil—a response to the supernatural. The castle used for the film was an actual building, not a set structure. In terms of action, the film is at times primitive; any psychological symbolism in it is more the retrospective invention of Kracauer than the actual intention of Murnau or Galeen at the time. Theodore Huff,[18] who researched Murnau's work carefully during the 1940s, writes of *Nosferatu*:

Its basis is in folklore, and Murnau unmistakably approached it as legend and fantasy, not psychological study. The characters have the simple, one-dimensional quality of legendary figures; the film is no more 'profound' than the American *Dracula* or *Franken-stein*. ... The acting style is very heavy, and the production obviously very cheap, some of the effects (such as the speeding up of the mysterious carriage by stop-motion, and the jerky opening and closing of phantom-controlled doors) seeming more ridiculous than weird.

Murnau followed this film with *Phantom* (1922), an adaptation from a novel by Gerhart Hauptmann, for which one of the script-writers was Thea von Harbou and one of the designers Warm. Huff derives the following description from a contemporary synopsis:

A humble town clerk longs to become a famous poet and marry a charming girl he has seen driving past him in a pony-drawn phaeton. Possessed by his longing, he sleeps with a prostitute resembling the unattainable girl and sinks ever deeper, until in the solitude of his prison cell he learns to renounce all phantoms. Murnau's film reached its pictorial climax with a montage sequence that fused street impressions into a vision of chaos.

After these two films, with their macabre expressionism, Murnau was to develop his work in other directions.

Expressionism, in its various forms and derivatives, was in effect finished in the German cinema by the mid 1920s, except for occasional last echoes, such as Alfred Abel's *Narcosis* (*Narkose*, 1929), which showed the subconscious images in the mind of a girl under an anaesthetic. In a treatment such as this, expressionism gives ground to more real psychological interests—the rational develop-ment of dream sequences introducing the non-rational symbols made familiar by Freud and the psychoanalysts' case work, the kind of images introduced by G. W. Pabst in his *Secrets of a Soul*, which will be discussed later. Ernö Metzner's [19] well-known film *Accident* (*Überfall*, 1929), could perhaps be called expressionist,

70, 71 *The Blue Angel* (*Der Blaue Engel*), 1930. Director, Joseph von Sternberg, with Emil Jannings and Marlene Dietrich.

72, 73 *The Blue Light* (*Das Blaue Licht*), 1932. Leni Riefenstahl, director and star.

74 *Kuhle Wampe*, 1932. Slatan Dudow, with Herta Thiele, Ernst Busch.

75 *The Threepenny Opera* (*Die Dreigroschenoper*), 1931. G. W. Pabst, with Rudolf Forster, Fritz Rasp, Reinhold Schünzel, Lotte Lenya, Ernst Busch, Valeska Gert.

76, 77 *Congress Dances* (*Der Kongress Tanzt*), 1931. Eric Charell, with Lilian Harvey, Willy Fritsch.

78 *The Flute Concert of Sanssouci* (*Das Flötenkonzert von Sanssouci*), 1930. Gustav Ucicky, with Otto Gebühr, Renate Müller.

79 *Three From the Petrol Pump* (*Drei von der Tankstelle*), 1930. Wilhelm Thiele, with Lilian Harvey, Willy Fritsch.

80 *Dawn* (*Morgenrot*), 1933. Gustav Ucicky, with Rudolf Forster, Adele Sandrock.

81 *Emil and the Detectives* (*Emil und die Detektive*), 1931. Gerhard Lamprecht, with Fritz Rasp.

82–84 *Girls in Uniform*
(*Mädchen in Uniform*),
1931. Leontine Sagan,
with Dorothea Wieck
and Herta Thiele.

85–88 *M*, (1931), Fritz Lang, with Peter Lorre.

89 *The Last Will of Dr Mabuse* (*Das Testament des Dr Mabuse*), 1933. G. W. Pabst, with Oskar Beregy, Rudolf Klein-Rogge.

90 *Westfront 1918*, 1930. G. W. Pabst, with Fritz Kampers, Gustav Diessl, Claus Clausen.

91 *Comradeship* (*Kameradschaft*), 1931. G. W. Pabst, with Alexander Granach, Fritz Kampers.

92–95 *Kameradschaft.*

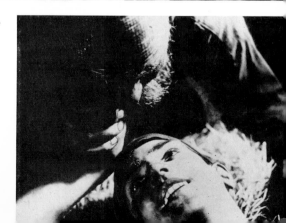

since it used distorting mirrors to create images supposed to reflect the mind of a man suffering from the after-effects of an accident. Many films introduced such momentary impressions of the un-balanced mind—they occur in *The Last Laugh* and in *Vaudeville*, for example. But in these films, the aim of which is psychological realism, however stylized pictorially, expressionism plays no real part.

Alongside the expressionist cinema, however, were the legendary costume films for which the German cinema was to be almost equally celebrated. These were the direct successors to the spectac-ular films, and they too gained immeasurably from the technical skills of the designers, set-builders, effects technicians and camera-men in the studios of the 1920s. Among the period films were *Fridericus Rex* (1923), directed by Arzen von Czerépy,[20] with Otto Gebühr projecting the legend rather than the actuality of the King, Murnau's screen version of *Tartuffe* (1925), scripted by Mayer from Molière, and Robison's *Manon Lescaut* (1927). These later period films were slow, stately and splendid when they were not merely decorative. The wholly legendary group included Arnold Fanck's *The Stone Rider* (*Der Steinerne Reiter*, 1923), Ludwig Berger's *Cinderella* (*Der Verlorene Schuh*, 1923), Arthur von Gerlach's *The Chronicle of the Grieshuus* (*Zur Chronik von Grieshuus*, 1923), and Murnau's *Faust*, with Emil Jannings. The legendary-historical figure of Frederick the Great proved an endless source for nationalist films; the first of these, directed by Czerépy, was *Sturm und Drang*; the second *Vater und Sohn*, both 1921. The following year came two further parts, *Sanssouci* and *Schicksalswende* (*Change of Fate*), which deal with the Seven Years' War and the death of Frederick. Otto Gebühr played Frederick throughout the series; indeed, he made the part his career, playing in film after film, both silent and sound.[21]

Tartuffe, with Emil Jannings, Lil Dagover and Werner Krauss, was a beautifully decorated production, turning Molière's satire on hypocrisy in French society into a much heavier Germanic version, with a quite unnecessary contemporary framing story in which a woman, a housekeeper, is the hypocrite, and the man, her master, the victim—until his eyes are opened by witnessing the story from Molière. The central story is spread over too extensive a canvas, and to counteract this Murnau uses large close-ups, particularly of

Jannings's burlesque, highly stylized acting as Tartuffe, a figure dressed entirely in black carrying a diminutive Bible. Murnau concentrated on the movements of his characters in the environment of the settings, insisting on mobile composition, balancing movement with space and its lighting, and featuring chosen objects of detail—Rotha, for example, pointed out, as others did at the time, the design of Oregon's ring, of the lace négligé in the final bedroom scene, the porcelain clock, and so forth. *Manon Lescaut*, designed for Robison by Paul Leni, also concentrated on close-ups of Manon (Lya de Putti) and her Chevalier (Vladimir Gaiderov), and, as Rotha says, the sets used had practical depth, so that the characters could pass down corridors and through doorways. Another, somewhat heavy and melodramatic silent film version of a classic was *Othello* (1922), directed by Dmitri Buchowetzki, with Emil Jannings as a staring, gesticulating, melodramatic Moor.

With the legendary film, the supernatural reappears. *Cinderella* is one of the near-perfect German films of the earlier 1920s, beautifully designed in a light baroque style by Rudolf Bamberger, who worked on his brother Ludwig Berger's [22] other films, *A Glass of Water* (*Ein Glas Wasser*, 1923), *The Waltz Dream* (*Ein Walzertraum*, 1925) and, after Berger's brief visit to Hollywood, *The Burning Heart* (*Das Brennende Herz*, 1929). *Cinderella*, with Helga Thomas and Paul Hartmann, remains in the memory for its consistently delicate pictorialism. Berger has a lighter touch than most of the German directors of the period, moving away from the macabre or the burlesque aspects of the supernatural into pure romanticism. Again, every composition was a study in symmetry, every figure posed, every movement thought of as a total pictorial composition. Kracauer may prefer to criticize such films as *Cinderella* as 'escapist', but it is a pure work of art, consistent and disciplined, with every right to exist in any age, troubled or otherwise. *The Chronicle of the Grieshuus*, with Lil Dagover and Paul Hartmann, has something of a Scandinavian quality and was notable for its use of locations in Schleswig, instead of relying on the resources of a studio. The script was by Thea von Harbou, which accounts for the melodrama in a story of unhappy love and fratricide. Ghosts haunt this family, who are themselves rather like apparitions in their great cloaks blown by the wind.

Faust, with the Swedish actor Gösta Ekman as Faust and, inevitably, Jannings as burlesque Mephisto, was to be Murnau's last
film before he left for the United States. Jannings stole the film,
conducting a humorous flirtation of his own with Marguerite's
aunt, Martha, played by the French *diseuse*, Yvette Guilbert. The
emotion of the Faust legend became lost in this much-developed
relationship under Murnau's solid pictorialism, at its best in the
medieval settings and the brilliantly evolved effects such as the
flight of Mephisto and Faust through the air over great tracts of model
landscapes and towns. Seymour Stern's [23] comment on a single scene
helps to visualize the technical skill with which the film was made:

The scene in *Faust* where the lovers pursue each other in a garden
is photographed from above. The audience sees Faust chasing
Marguerite down a path lined with flowers, the scene is pretty,
amorous; but the angle at which it is taken gives it the particular
quality which relates it to *Faust*, so that the sequence could not be
lifted out of that film and patched into another; the scene is taken
from the point of view where Mephisto is watching the two puppets
who are innocent of his power over them. The spectators do not see
Mephisto; but they see with his eyes, and it is the angle which gives
them the sense of impending tragedy, which corrupts the innocence
and charm of the little scene played before them.

In 1925 Murnau had made a very different film, *The Last Laugh*
(*Der Letzte Mann*, literally, 'The Last Man') which was to form
part of the new, stylized realism characteristic of another, even
more important, phase in the German silent cinema. The script was
by Carl Mayer, who had already written a considerable number of
films which in one way or another anticipated his very significant
contribution to this outstanding film, the most fruitful of all his
many collaborations with Murnau. He had written the script for
Walk in the Night (*Der Gang in Die Nacht*, 1921), featuring Conrad
Veidt, the story of a doctor who restores the sight of an artist only
to find that his wife becomes the artist's mistress. The climax
involves the wife pleading for her lover when his sight fails for the
second time. In the same year Mayer had also written *The Haunted
Castle* (*Schloss Vogelöd*), a film in the Swedish style about a young
couple living in a castle in an atmosphere of tension. In the same
busy period another film was produced from a Mayer script, Leopold

Jessner's[24] *Backstairs* (*Hintertreppe*) with Henny Porten, Fritz Kortner and Wilhelm Dieterle, a violent melodrama of a maidservant who believes herself deserted by her lover because an unbalanced postman, a cripple, intercepts his letter out of jealousy and finally kills him, which in turn leads to the girl's suicide. In all these films Mayer showed an increasing interest in problems of individual psychology and relationships.

Far more important than *Backstairs*, which remained a melodrama in its essentials, were two films Mayer scripted for the actor-director Lupu Pick: *Shattered* (*Scherben*, 1921, with Werner Krauss) and *New Year's Eve* (*Sylvester*, 1923).[25] In the first of these Mayer and Pick experimented with the idea of trying to make a film without titles or captions, the whole narration carried by the mime. There is, in fact, one sentence put on the screen: 'I am a murderer'. This is said at the end of the film by Werner Krauss in the part of a railway track-walker who lives in extreme isolation with his wife and daughter and murders his daughter's seducer, a railway inspector. The track-walker stops an express in order to confess to the engine-driver what he has done. He is met with complete indifference, but his daughter commits suicide. According to Kracauer, this story reveals the disintegration of society, a theme revived in the other film directed by Lupu Pick, *New Year's Eve*, in which a married man proves too immature to assert his authority in the disputes which divide his mother and his wife. His dependence on his mother is shown to be pathological and results in his suicide. The climax comes on New Year's Eve, when the crowds are celebrating. They are as indifferent to his troubles as nature itself, which is shown throughout the film as serene and untroubled by man's self-destructive passions. The action of *New Year's Eve* was concentrated into a single night; that of *Shattered* into three days.

These films, as we have seen, were usually termed *Kammerspiel-filme* (intimate films); they developed into psychological studies, in which a close view of the action enabled every nuance of expression to be seen. Pick himself, in his introduction to the published script of *Sylvester*, wrote:

Carl Mayer calls Sylvester a *Lichtspiel* (a play of light). . . . No doubt he wanted to indicate the change of light and shade in human soul, light and darkness for ever interchanging in human relationships. At any rate, that is how I interpret it. Certainly, in the course of directing this film, it was increasingly clear to me, from day to day, that here was a subject in which universal values were masterfully compressed within the events of a single hour. . . . It stirs emotions common to us all. While watching these three persons wounding each other in the narrow confines of their world . . . we see also all the jubilation going on around them. . . . The surrounding world, though not involved in the action, plays an important part.

The climax of Carl Mayer's work in Germany was *The Last Laugh*. Emil Jannings appeared, at the age of thirty-nine, in what might be considered his finest character performance in silent films—as the old hotel doorman demoted because of his age from his seemingly grand, uniformed position at the revolving door of an international hotel to the degrading work of a white-coated lavatory attendant in the bowels of the building. For Carl Mayer, Murnau and their cameraman, Karl Freund, this became an exercise in visual tragedy to be achieved entirely by means of stylization of setting, lighting, camera-treatment and acting. Mayer's script slowly, inevitably and ironically detailed the psychological collapse which his demotion brings about in this huge man, whose whole status in the world, both inside and outside the hotel, in his public and in his private life, depends on the ankle-length, metal-buttoned, gold-braided greatcoat and peaked cap, the uniform of the hotel doorman, which does not even belong to him. When this is taken off his back his social status collapses; he is mocked and disowned by his relatives, who were once so proud of him; the whole district where he lives derides him; the women who competed to catch his eye laugh at him. His demotion is also theirs. From being a proud, upright, heavy-paced man, the wielder of the luggage of the great, he shrinks into a diminished figure, old and bent, sidling down the steps, carrying his stack of towels into the abyss of the men's washroom.

Like *Sylvester*, this film has a single caption, which arrives like a trumpet-blast and announces Mayer's tailpiece, a satiric happy end designed to end all other happy ends. The author's manuscript is seen in the typewriter, and the words are tapped out: 'Here at the scene of his last disgrace the old man will slowly pine away, and the story would really have ended there had not the author taken pity on the forsaken old man and added an epilogue in which he makes things happen as, unfortunately, they do not happen in real life.' So we see the demoted porter when he has at last come into his own; he has inherited a fortune bequeathed him by an eccentric American millionaire, since it was the lavatory attendant who was the last person to tend him when he died. Now he becomes the guest who has to be honoured in the hotel restaurant—except, of course, that the socialites laugh at him behind his back because he does not know how to behave. He leaves with his friend, the old night-watchman, showering gold upon the world, drawn in a coach-and-four.

Theodore Huff's analysis of Murnau's technique in the realization of Mayer's script is worth recalling:

In *The Last Laugh* the camera travels almost continuously. In an opening scene of sheer magic it rides down the elevator and moves through the hotel lobby to the revolving door (a leit motif of the film); it walks through doors and windows; it characterises, emotes, moves as freely as the actors. When the old doorman gets drunk at the wedding feast, the camera bounces around the room instead (the cameraman was actually on roller skates). The subjective use of the camera is brought to a climax in this film. It gave the camera a new dominant prestige.

Mayer used a straightforward, fluid method of narration. A psychological study of human values is rendered simply without subplots, and the technique of 'moving in' from long-shot to close-up, rather than 'cutting', carried out the spirit of the script—and though picturemakers were to find that imitation of this technique was not suitable for all stories, here it achieved a perfect continuity. *The Last Laugh* is an example of almost pure cinema; in it Murnau broke entirely the stranglehold of stage technique.

Other interesting aspects of the film include the expressive sets of a universal, de-nationalized city with depth achieved by forced perspectives; the lighting (especially in the basement scenes and the 'night-to-morning' effects in the slum quarters); the revolving door and swinging glass doors, symbolizing the endless revolution of life and fortune; the famous dream sequence with its multiple exposures, distorting lenses, slow motion and stylized figures, and where, true to dream psychology(?) locales are superimposed (the hotel lobby becomes surrounded and confused by the slum court); the use of ceilings on some sets; and, in general, perfection of detail and composition pervaded by an overall poetic quality. The epilogue,

38

incidentally, contains what would now be known as a 'Russian Montage' sequence though it was made before *Potemkin*. It contains a 'montage' of laughing faces, of approximately a second or less each (actual number of frames: 20, 22, 24, 21, 16, 19, 14, 15, 22, 29).

During the period when Carl Mayer was scripting these *Kammerspiel* films, others were made which took the melodramatic situations arising from love and jealousy and gave them a psychological emphasis which made them memorable. The first was *The Street* (*Die Strasse*, 1923), scripted and directed by Karl Grune,[26] who, according to the historian, Carl Vincent, acquired his initial interest in the cinema as a result of living among foreign soldiers during the war whose language he never learned and with whom he had to maintain contact by gesture and by watching their facial expressions. It was this prolonged experience of wordless communication which brought him into film-making. *The Street* was in consequence made without captions, like the films of Mayer; a middle-aged man (played by Eugen Kloepfer), bored with his wife, deserts her in order to experience the joys of the street at night. He and another victim, a rich man from the provinces, are robbed by a prostitute and her male 'protectors'. After a game of cards, the provincial is killed and his companion framed as the murderer by the men from the underworld. Finally released by the police after a confession by the real murderer, the man who left his wife returns to her for good, his experience of the street having been enough for him. Kloepfer plays his part with stylized realism, a bridge between the fashionable expressionistic acting and a form of concentrated, well-marked realism of the kind Pabst was to favour. At the same time, the realism of the street is a 'heightened' one, stylized by the play of light, moving shadows, and darkness, while the wanderer himself suffers hallucinations which imply the nihilistic hell of the vicious world to which he is submitting his innocence.

The seeker after forbidden experience is a woman in Paul Czinner's[27] film *Nju* (1924), the first in which his wife, Elisabeth Bergner, was to feature. Nju leaves her vulgar husband (played by Jannings) and her child to pursue an alluring stranger (Veidt) with whom she enjoys a period of love in a furnished room until he deserts her. Elisabeth Bergner proved to have a special, temperamental gift for portraying suppressed, nervous femininity. Nju in the end drowns herself. The film was filled with a melancholy, romantic fatalism—love, the great dream, becomes love, the nightmare. In films where the situation did not lead to these acts of tragic disillusion, its sensual demands produced jealousy and violence as a result of such triangular relationships as that in Dupont's [28] *Vaudeville* (*Variété*, 1925), with Emil Jannings and Lya de Putti, a film based on a novel by Felix Holländer. This film uses a conventional flashback—a murderer, pardoned because of his quiet submission to authority (symbolized by endless, almost slow-motion shots of Jannings' bent back revealing its huge convict's number), tells the prison governor the full story behind the killing, a *crime passionel*. Jannings then turns into the breezy, unsuspicious sensualist, Huller, who succumbs to the sexuality of an oriental type of girl he hires for his travelling show. He deserts his shabby, worn-out wife and takes his new mistress on tour as his partner in a trapeze act. When they achieve some success and are invited to become the partners of an international star of the trapeze, Artinelli, the inevitable happens—the girl prefers the lean, suave, smiling acrobat to her heavy-going middle-aged lover. Huller, in his jealousy, kills Artinelli by intentionally missing his grasp during a triple somersault at the Berlin Wintergarten. Then, very slowly and deliberately, he surrenders himself to the police. Helped by his cameraman, Freund, Dupont used the camera with a fluidity which was an innovation in 1925; there is almost a quality of *cinévérité* about its intrusiveness. Kracauer quotes an interview given by Freund in America in 1937: 'In *Variété*,' he said, 'the unaccustomed angle was stressed by necessity, owing to cramped quarters in the Berlin Winter Garden, where the picture was made, and this film, curiously enough, was an original source-book of the lying-on-the-stomach school of photography, which has today reached the proportion of a national craze.' The camera swings with an acrobat's-eye-view of the spectators in the Wintergarten; the viewer is made to feel part of the act which is taking place.

In a class of her own was Asta Nielsen, the greatest actress of the German silent cinema. After establishing herself, as we have seen, before the First World War, she appeared in a great variety of films during the 1920s, including Sven Gade's *Hamlet* (1920),

Downfall (*Absturz*, 1923), *Hedda Gabler* (1924), Bruno Rahn's *The Tragedy of the Street* (*Dirnentragödie*, 1927), *The Lusts of Mankind* (*Laster der Menschheit*, 1927), as well as in Pabst's *The Joyless Street* (1925), which is described later. The first was a new story, adapted not from Shakespeare but from Nordic sources, with Asta Nielsen in male dress as Hamlet. This heavily literary film did not show her to best advantage. In *Downfall* she brings a wonderful life and pathos to the conventional figure of the elderly prostitute abandoned for a young whore by a youth she wants to help and whom she believes to be in love with her. She incites her 'protector' to kill the girl, but in the end kills herself, while the boy returns to the shelter of his mother's arms. Asta Nielsen specialized in outcast women, whom she played with great sympathy, even with a certain majesty, giving them the enrichment of character which came from her own greatness as an actress.

With G. W. Pabst,[29] an Austrian from Vienna, the new realism in the German cinema found its master. He came to the cinema as the romantic pessimist, and after making a period film, *The Treasure* (*Der Schatz*, 1923), which revealed nothing of his potential talent, he showed his real powers in his first great film, *The Joyless Street* (*Die Freudlose Gasse*, 1925), adapted from a story by Hugo Bettauer. Set in post-war Vienna during the period of the inflation, it shows what happened to a middle-class family when its head, Councillor Rumfort, loses his money. His daughter, played by Greta Garbo (the only part she played in a German film), becomes a cabaret dancer who declines into prostitution. The family, destitute but determined to uphold the old bourgeois values, are forced to live upon her earnings. The inflation draws a ruthless line between the profiteers and exploiters, who discard all human values, and those who fall victim to these new and unknown conditions. Crowds queue for meat, while the sadistic butcher, played by Werner Krauss, exudes power with his great white hound and his vicious favouritism in the distribution of meat. The total effect of this film is of realism undiluted by any form of studio aestheticism; rather, the photography by Guido Seeber turns the studio into a lazar house, emphasizing filth and depravity to the point of melodrama. Nevertheless, the impact of these films after the expressionist and decorative work of other directors was of a ruthless, stark power which sent the censors hurrying to their scissors. Asta Nielsen appears as a 'kept woman', who is driven to murder for her lover; in some versions her part was erased.[30]

The Joyless Street is not a perfect film; the melodramatic touches of which critics complained at the time intrude on the realism of much of Pabst's earlier work. However beautifully played by Asta Nielsen, the character of the prostitute she portrays is essentially theatrical, while at the last moment Pabst rescues Rumfort and his daughter with the help of a lieutenant from the American Red Cross. But the central core of the film had a truthfulness new to the cinema; there is no film of the period with which it can be compared except, perhaps, Stroheim's *Greed* (1924), completed just before it and treated, in this case by its producers, with equal disrespect.

Pabst's next film of importance was *Secrets of a Soul* (*Geheimnisse einer Seele*, 1926), a film intended to dramatize a case from the records of psycho-analysis. It was prepared with the help of two of Freud's assistants, Dr Hanns Sachs and Dr Karl Abraham. The central character is a professor (Werner Krauss) [31] who consults a psycho-analyst because he has in a dream attempted to stab his wife and found on waking that his actions are deeply and inexplicably inhibited, and that he feels compelled to commit the crime of which he has dreamed. The rest of the film is derived from the interviews with his analyst, looking back to elements in his dream and the memories he recalls of youthful jealousy of the mutual attraction he observed then between his future wife and a handsome cousin, which has led to his impotence during their married life. The film is made as nearly like a scientific documentary as possible for the period; it is coolly observant rather than dramatically involved, but even here Pabst felt the need to soften the film with a happy end: at the close we see the professor in a mountain scene, holding a baby.

After *Secrets of a Soul*, Pabst made *The Love of Jeanne Ney* (*Die Liebe der Jeanne Ney*, 1927), derived in a somewhat bowdlerized form from the political novel by Ilya Ehrenburg, novelist and Russian Soviet journalist based at the time in Paris. Jeanne Ney (Edith Jehanne of France) is French and bourgeois; Andreas, her lover (Unc Henning of Sweden), is a young Russian Communist whom she first meets in the Crimea during the period of the civil war; her father is murdered there for political reasons by one of Andreas's comrades. Nevertheless, their love flowers in Paris, where Andreas is sent by the authorities. But wherever they are, a sadistic anti-Communist agent, Khabiliev (Fritz Rasp of Germany), haunts and frustrates them, eventually murdering Jeanne's uncle after betraying his blind daughter (Brigitte Helm), to whom he has proposed marriage, and contriving that Andreas shall be regarded as the murderer. However, unlike the novel, the film has a happy end; Pabst's instructions from UFA were to try to make the film in the American style; more nearly he made it, when he could, in the Russian, since Eisenstein's film *The Battleship Potemkin* was enjoying a great vogue in Berlin during 1926. The film develops into something of a social document exposing Europe's decadence. Pabst used a highly mobile, almost free-style camera treatment of every action in the interests of realism, instructing his camera-director, Fritz Arno Wagner, to avoid artificiality in lighting and effects, and achieving at least as much through skilful cutting as he does from the visual impact of individual shots. The skill of the camera-work lies in its smooth fluidity, tracking, panning, moving with people or, as Rotha puts it, 'nosing' its way into angles and corners. *The Love of Jeanne Ney* contains the most advanced editing so far achieved in the German cinema, and demonstrates still further the influence of *The Battleship Potemkin* and the montage theory of editing put forward by the leading Russian film-makers. Nevertheless, the film has its melodramatic and sentimental touches, even suggesting that Andreas, the communist, may become a convert to the Catholic faith.[32]

Interviewed by Kenneth Macpherson, editor of *Close-Up*, Pabst said in 1927: 'You have no idea how difficult it is for us to make good pictures, of how I had to *fight* to make this picture. It is really terrible. They want us to make only films in the American style. . . . To make American pictures we must *be* American in our mind, and that we cannot be.' Of the church scene, which was so much criticized, but which Macpherson praises as 'a scene full of warmth and deep feeling', Pabst said: 'All they have said is that a Communist would not go to church. I say to them, "I am showing that this Communist *does* go to church." "Oh, but a Communist doesn't go to church." "Well, I am showing you *how* this Communist did go to church." '

Crisis (*Abwege*, 1928) followed, starring Brigitte Helm; this is the story of a rich middle-class woman who out of boredom with her husband joins with others of the same class as herself to forget their hatred of life through the practice of sexual excesses. It developed into one of Pabst's more subtly understanding films about women; he and Lubitsch were the first great directors of women, giving stature to actresses who were either unknown (such as Garbo), or ill-used in other films (such as Brigitte Helm), or who had totally unknown qualities ready to be revealed, like Louise Brooks, whom Pabst was to bring from America for his next film, *Pandora's Box* (*Die Büchse der Pandora*, 1929), derived from Franz Wedekind's plays *Erdgeist* and *Pandora's Box*. Louise Brooks plays Lulu, a young prostitute driven to self-destruction by sexual need, a destruction which engulfs the succession of men with whom she is involved. This most extraordinary film has been compared with Carl Dreyer's *Passion of Joan of Arc* (France, 1928) for the intense, intimate way it uses the camera to watch the processes of thought and feeling through close shots of the face. In the final stages of the film the man the girl is drawn to proves to be Jack the Ripper. Until this moment, her love for a man dies with his physical exhaustion, and it is then that she had been impelled by disgust to destroy him. Now she herself faces destruction. This film was criticized (by Rotha, among others) for its innate inability through lack of sound to match Wedekind's revealing dialogue to the pathetic innocence of Lulu's appearance, which is so much at variance with the sexuality of what she says.

In the spring of 1929 Pabst hurried off for a five-month location in the Alps to make another silent film along with Arnold Fanck,[33] *The White Hell of Pitz Palü* (*Die Weisse Hölle von Pitz Palü*, 1929), in which Leni Riefenstahl appeared. Ernst Udet, the air ace, was to help to photograph the mountain ascents as well as appear in the film; it presented the story of the rescue of a young couple trapped by an avalanche while climbing Pitz Palü on their honeymoon. The film was later issued with a simple synchronized soundtrack.

Pabst's last silent film was *The Diary of a Lost Girl* (*Tagebuch einer Verlorenen*, 1929), another study of a sexually obsessed girl,

Thymian (played by Louise Brooks), whose seduction by her father's evil-minded assistant (played by Fritz Rasp) eventually leads her to prostitution and to a reform school run by a sadistic governess (Valeska Gert) who beats time with a spoon while the girls feed and do their exercises like women in a concentration camp.

Interest in the effects which could be achieved on the screen not only from photographic lighting and composition but also from editing was not confined to the dramatic feature film. On a more mundane level Germany was far more developed in what came to be called later the documentary film, not only in its direct use for education, but in the general sense of producing endless 'Kultur-filme', which were 'interest' films about science, travel, physical culture, art and architecture, industry and so forth. The *Kulturfilme* were often suitable for entertainment in the theatres. The film was also beginning to be used for propaganda in the political field, as we shall see; both the growing Nazi party and the Communists were producing films for their rallies and election meetings towards the close of the 1920s. The arrival in Germany of such outstanding Russian films as *The Battleship Potemkin* and, later, *Mother* and *October*, drew attention to the possibilities of 'montage', or creative editing, which might more readily be applied experimentally to documentaries than to the commercial feature film.

In Germany, therefore, an avant-garde film movement began, not on the same scale as the parallel movement in France, but not un-related to it. The most celebrated of German documentaries of the 1920s is *Berlin, Symphony of a Great City* (*Berlin, Die Symphonie einer Grosstadt*, 1927), a joint creative venture of Carl Mayer, who conceived the idea of creating a 'melody of pictures' out of the movement and pulse of life in Berlin, Karl Freund, the great cinematographer, and Walter Ruttmann,[34] who edited the vast quantity of material Freund and others shot round Mayer's basic script. The film was assembled and cut with a potential music score by Edmund Meisel very much in mind; Meisel had produced the stirring score used in Germany for *The Battleship Potemkin*, so stirring, indeed, that the film was banned. Paul Rotha, who became a close friend of Mayer when the screen-writer finally settled in England to work on documentary, has revealed that Mayer had wearied of the artificiality of studio production and had longed to breathe the freer air which actuality film-making seemed to represent. The result was a feature-length impressionistic study of Berlin from dawn to dusk assembled from the vast footage supplied by Freund and his colleagues. In an interview for *Close-Up*, Freund revealed that he had the sensitivity of the film stock he used increased in order to achieve 'candid-camera' and *cinévérité* results in any degree of lighting, and that he used various devices to conceal the camera from his subjects. This, he claimed, was 'photography in its purest form'. Ruttmann, who had made a number of abstract films, was biased in the direction of creating fluid patterns out of the infinite number of plastic compositions that city photography inevitably created, making mobile patterns out of machine-movements and the like, and under his influence something of Mayer's original intention—the rhythm of life in a city rather than its more physical plasticity—was lost. Meisel provided the orchestral score, a piano version of which has fortunately survived, written in a contemporary idiom and carefully cued to individual sequences and shots.[35] Kurt London, however, in his book *Film Music* (1936) considered that Meisel ruined the effect of the film with his 'harsh atonalities'; nevertheless, Meisel must be recognized as Germany's pioneer in composing music for films. Of his score for *The Battleship Potemkin*, London wrote less than ten years later, after Meisel's premature death:

His expressionistic style, turning first and foremost on rhythm, was many stages in advance of the films for which he composed. His musical accompaniment for the Russian film *Battleship Potemkin* marked him out as a pioneer in film music. The film made a deep impression wherever it was shown, but there is no doubt that this impression was to no small extent enhanced by the music. It is significant that several European countries which allowed the film itself to pass the censor forbade the music to be played. Its really provocative rhythm was liable to lash the revolutionary instincts latent in audiences to boiling-point. It was reminiscent of that classical example of a revolution caused by music—the riot which resulted from the performance of Auber's *La Muette de Portici*. The rhythms which mark the departure of the mutinous ship, as the engines begin to move, have become famous, and have since been imitated countless times.

The music for the film *Potemkin* was Meisel's masterpiece.

Mayer, in the end, found *Berlin* superficial—and no doubt because of this quality its popularity, and that of its successors and imitators, was assured. Ruttmann went on to make other 'symphonies', in Düsseldorf for example. Wilfried Basse made *Street Markets in Berlin*, at times introducing stop motion and 'freezing' the action; another film portrayed life in terms of reportage—*People on Sunday* (*Menschen am Sonntag*, 1929), remarkable for the future glitter of the names of those who collaborated on it, including Robert Siodmak, Billy Wilder and Fred Zinnemann, as well as the cinematographer, Eugen Schüftan. In the film a number of different people are followed through their Sunday on a lakeside near Berlin. Other documentary films included *Adventures of a Ten Mark Note* (*Abenteuer eines 10-Mark Schein*), directed by Ruttmann, and *Ways to Strength and Beauty* (*Wege zur Kraft und Schönheit*) by Nicolas Kaufmann.

By now the film was being recognized for its social-political as well as for its artistic value. Various associations were formed to encourage liberal-leftist and avant-garde interest in the film, such as the Popular Association for Film Art (Volksverband für Filmkunst, 1928) and the German League for the Independent Film (Deutsche Liga für Unabhängigen Film). Inserts were used, too, in the theatre, for example by the celebrated leftist stage director, Erwin Piscator.

The avant-garde can be seen at its most characteristic in Ernö Metzner's film already mentioned—*Accident* (*Überfall*, 1929). Kenneth Macpherson enthusiastically described this film for *Close-Up* (April 1929):

Überfall is a short film of 460 metres, and its cost was roughly £100. It is the story simply of a man who wins some marks in a gambling saloon, is attacked by a footpad, taken to hospital unconscious, and in the end comes to. The greater part of the film is occupied with his dream while in a state of anaesthesia.

It was this part of the film that we were enabled to see while in Berlin, the remainder at that time, not having yet been finished. It is as vivid and extraordinary a piece of work as has yet in this way been done. We say broadly 'in this way' to embrace abstraction, impressionism, and straight narrative—a somewhat formidable combination.

It is extraordinary, for while it is composed entirely of fantasy, it is obviously a dream fantasy, and one influenced by some remote consciousness of the actual events going on around. That is to say, that while its dimension is strictly Freudian, and made up of nightmare images, this being the *real* (as opposed to the ghostly); the impression is given that 'real-life' (the hospital, the surgeon, nurses, etc.) are the remote, or ghostly dimension. To describe how this impression is conveyed would perhaps be impossible, since no indication is given in the actual images except of the troubled subconscious of the drugged patient. The raising of a finger, to receive balanced on its tip a mark piece which sways vertiginously to it, only to vanish at the moment of contact is sufficiently in the foreground of all psychoanalytical text-books to need no definition here. Its constant recurrence throughout the dream, like a task or exercise constantly interrupted, is a punctuation that removes any ambiguity.

Dr. Hanns Sachs, the eminent Viennese psycho-analyst, was present at the same showing, and expressed his great satisfaction at both the scientific and artistic value of the fragment. It is extremely well photographed. It is extremely beautiful. It moves with both fascination and grace. It is an important film, because it is the sort of film that much might be written about, having much to give. The flow of images is sonorous, tightens the mind to receive the exact impression of anaesthetic—the constant turning over and over, and repeating of something that becomes horror by its repetition alone. This is valuable, and has something to say, and (to repeat) something to give.

In 1948 Hans Richter, then in the United States, wrote his own personal account of the work in abstract animation that he and the Swedish painter Viking Eggeling had conducted in Germany after a considerable period of experimentation going back to 1918. He wrote of Eggeling's work, the first of its kind in abstract animation:

His drawings stunned me with their extraordinary logic and beauty, a new beauty. He used *contrasting* elements to *dramatize* two (or more) complexes of forms and used *analogies* in these same complexes to *relate* them again. In varying proportions, number, intensity, position, etc., new contrasts and new analogies were born in perfect order, until there grew a kind of 'functioning' between the different form units, which made you feel movement, rhythm, continuity ... as clear as in Bach. That's what I saw immediately!

We decided to work together and Eggeling came with me to Germany where we lived and co-operated for the following three years.

48

Our mutual interest and understanding led to a great number of variations on one theme or another, usually on small sheets of paper which we arranged on the floor in order to study their relationship and to find out their most logical and convincing continuity, their maximum of (emotional) meaning. One day we decided to establish a definite form of continuity in a definite way: on scrolls. This step saved us first of all the pain of creeping over the floor, but it gave us something else: a new form of expression (used 4000 B.C. already). In these scrolls we tried to build different phases of transformation as if they were phrases of a symphony or fugue. Eggeling's first scroll was a 'Horizontal-Vertical Mass' early in 1919, or late in 1918. Mine, at the same time, a 'Prelude' on the theme of 'Crystallization'. Despite the fact that the scroll did not contain more than eight or ten characteristic transformations of a theme it became evident to us that these scrolls, as a whole, implied movement ... and movement implied film! We had to try to realize this implication.

Not many had ever come into the film so unexpectedly. We did not know more about cameras than we had seen in shop windows, and the mechanized technique of photography frightened us.

One day in 1920 UFA allowed us to use their animation tables. We made a tryout with one figure of my scroll, 'Prelude'. It took the UFA technician more than a week to animate, haphazardly, the complicated drawing (about thirty feet long).

In more orthodox animation the outstanding film-maker in Germany was to be Lotte Reiniger,[36] pioneer in silhouette animation whose first film was a Chinese fairy tale, *The Flying Suitcase* (*Der Fliegende Koffer*, 1921). Her best-known films in the silent period were *The Adventures of Prince Achmed* (*Die Geschichte des Prinzen Achmid*, 1926) and the series, *Dr Dolittle and his Animals* (*Dr Dolittle und seine Tiere*, 1927 – 28). She adapted the ancient technique of the Chinese shadow theatres, so popular in eighteenth-century France, to the medium of the film. Her films were painstaking in their craftsmanship, so that the movement of her jointed, flat-figure marionettes became full of character, charm and beautifully devised mime. They were, in fact, most carefully choreographed. But, like all animation, her work was to be seen to its best advantage after the coming of sound, as in her beautiful film, *Papageno* (1935), choreographed to the music of Mozart.

Chapter three

The sound film
before Hitler

It was only to be expected that Germany's technicians would play a key part in bringing optical sound to the cinema. The earlier attempts at synchronization, in which Messter had been among the pioneers, failed because adequate amplification of sound reproduced through the gramophone proved impossible in theatre conditions. Other attempts, including a system similar to the pianola, also proved inadequate.

It was the three German innovators Vogt, Engl and Massolle who adopted an entirely new approach—stemming from experiments carried out in Britain and elsewhere during the previous fifty years—and reproduced sound in terms of light. The German pioneers developed a system known as Tri-Ergon as early as 1918, which was to lead to recording sound photographically (or optically) on film; parallel developments were taking place in the United States where Lee de Forrest demonstrated his Phonofilm in 1923. The Warner Brothers in the United States were already demonstrating film accompanied by synchronized disc recordings, and Fox acquired the rights to both the Tri-Ergon and the Phonofilm systems. While Warner Brothers popularized sound films through synchronization with disc, as in *The Jazz Singer* (1927), Fox developed optical sound with Fox Movietone News in the same year. The disc system of sound reproduction gradually gave way to the optical system, Warner presenting *The Lights of New York* by this method in July 1928.

In Germany, UFA had held the licence for Tri-Ergon from 1923 to 1926, but had done little with it. The impetus had passed to the United States, though the rights in Europe were taken over in 1928 by a new company, Tobis (Ton-Bild-Syndikat A.G.), which in 1929 combined with Klang Film, a company set up by the electrical trust, A.E.G. and Siemens. This combine, Tobis-Klangfilm, was sufficiently strong to fight the American combination of Warners and Fox for the German patent rights. The German sound film was free to develop on its own terms. The progressive ratio of the production of sound to silent film in German studios is interesting: September 1929, 3 per cent sound; January 1930, 30 per cent sound; September 1930, 84 per cent sound. The first German feature film exploiting sound was *I Kiss Your Hand, Madame* (*Ich küsse ihre Hand, Madame*, 1929), which featured Marlene Dietrich, popular in cabaret and, to a lesser degree, in silent film, and Harry Liedtke who, like Jolson in *The Jazz Singer*, actually sang from the screen. It was closely followed by Ruttmann's *Melody of the World* (*Die Melodie der Welt*, March 1929), a film sponsored by the Hamburg-Amerika line. Ruttmann's film proved to be visually impressive but socially superficial; it was a 'symphony' of library material purporting to show mankind's 'behaviour' seen in various aspects: conventional love, religious practice, death and burial, movement and travel, warfare and so forth. From the point of view of the sponsors, it offered a cross-section of the world served by their liners. Its original score by Wolfgang Zeller is described by Kurt London in *Film Music* as 'naturally 232', but beyond the music, Ruttmann exploited to the full the rhythmic possibilities of actual sounds with ships' sirens, anchor-chains, and the pulse of the liners' engines.[1] The film was followed by E. A. Dupont's fully developed 'talkie' (or dialogue film), *Atlantic*, made at Elstree studios in Britain, with a German-language version of a story showing the inevitable disaster overtaking the passengers on a luxury liner at sea. The way was open for the dialogue film to flourish, and for such light operatic musicals as Wilhelm Thiele's *Three from the Petrol Pump* (*Drei von der Tankstelle*, 1930), the first film to star Lilian Harvey (a British actress who went to work in German films) and Willy Fritsch, Eric Charell's *Congress Dances* (*Der Kongress Tanzt*, 1931) also with Lilian Harvey and Willy Fritsch, *The Private Secretary* (*Die Privatsekretärin*, 1931),[2] with Renate Müller, and Ludwig Berger's *War of the Waltzes* (*Walzerkrieg*, 1933). These films were in part inspired by the success in Germany of René Clair's early operetta films, and were themselves often cinematically inventive as well as very entertaining.

Erich Pommer, at Jannings's suggestion, invited Josef von

Sternberg[3] to Germany after he had completed *Thunderbolt*, his first sound film in Hollywood, to direct *The Blue Angel* (*Der Blaue Engel*, 1930) in both English and German dialogue versions. This was based on Heinrich Mann's novel, *Professor Unrath*, and told the story of the downfall of an elderly schoolmaster (Jannings) who conceives a self-destructive passion for Lola, a cabaret singer (Marlene Dietrich). The story is melodramatic in the old style of *Vaudeville*, but Sternberg and the composer, Friedrich Holländer, brought distinction to the way in which the sound was handled. John Huntley has described the use of music and musical motifs in this film, in *The Technique of Film Music*:

The musical score, by Friedrich Holländer, consists of the main theme songs, sung by Marlene Dietrich, including *Falling in Love Again* and *Blonde Women*, and various settings of a German chorale (cf. the bird-catcher's theme from Mozart's *The Magic Flute*— Papageno's tune). There is no 'background' music as such, although the film has an Overture for the opening titles, consisting of an arrangement of *Falling in Love Again* and the Chorale tune.

From then on, music is used naturalistically. The professor (Emil Jannings) whistles a few notes from the Chorale tune to the bird cage as he takes breakfast. The elaborate chiming clock over the gates of the University also plays the same tune as the clock strikes eight. In the Blue Angel café, the stage band punctuates the action realistically, even to the extent of being motivated by doors opening and closing as the stage area is approached. Marlene Dietrich's songs are, of course, naturalistic. In the class-room scene, children's voices start and end as a window is opened and closed.

The Professor arrives at the door of the University. He pulls a bell cord and the bell sounds inside. A limping caretaker, with a bull's-eye torch, opens the door. The Professor brushes past him and goes upstairs to his old classroom. As he enters, a very quiet sound of a slow string bass beat is heard, gradually swelling to a sustained, expanding string tremolo that covers scenes of the care-taker coming up to the door and entering the room. He finds the Professor dead at his old desk, his hand gripping the front edge as he lies in an attitude of desperation. The music resolves into the Chorale tune, the main melody picked out on muffled chimes against a background of flowing strings and harp arpeggios. The film ends in a long tracking shot back through the classroom as the clock outside strikes twelve.

Marlene Dietrich, the daughter of a Prussian police officer, had trained in Reinhardt's theatre school in 1921 before starting her career. Sternberg, who saw her in a cabaret show, recognized the potentialities of her beauty and insisted, against considerable opposition, on giving her the star role in the film. He changed her screen image entirely, as she acknowledged in an interview she gave after she had left Germany and accompanied Sternberg to the United States: 'Von Sternberg found me in Germany,' she said. 'I was nothing there. He believed in me, worked with me, trained me— he gave all his knowledge, experience and energy to make me a success. . . . He made me over.'

Another unusual film threaded through with songs appeared during the following years, the Russian Alexis Granowski's *Song of Life* (*Das Lied von Leben*)—a film which attacked bourgeois society and had as its climax a Caesarian operation on a young girl who had run away from a society marriage and married a young worker who had rescued her from suicide. It was vaguely idealistic, an attempt perhaps to answer the growing menace to democratic rule in Germany offered by the great rival factions of the Communists and the National Socialists. With the economic crisis American aid to Germany had suddenly been withdrawn and, as in other countries, widespread unemployment followed upon the recession in industry. The musicals, the escapist films, and the 'good luck' films with fantasy transformations from rags to riches, such as *Congress Dances*, filled the German screens. In *The Man without a Name* (*Mensch ohne Namen*, 1932) Werner Krauss played an industrialist whose amnesia contracted in war deprives him of his identity; nevertheless, he is saved from suicide and the film ends happily for him with a new career and a new marriage. Lupu Pick's last film before he died of gastric poisoning, *Streetsong* (*Gassenhauer*, 1931), shows how a group of unemployed musicians win success with a song. More melancholy, in the older style, because the excesses of passion lead to downfall and suicide, were two outstandingly well made films by Paul Czinner, featuring his wife, Elisabeth Bergner—*Ariane* (1931) and *Dreaming Lips* (*Der Träumende Mund*, 1932); in the latter a wife, torn between maintaining her marriage and an obsessive love for a great violinist, ends up by drowning herself. Carl Mayer wrote the scripts for both these films. Soon, in 1932, he came to settle in London, where he was to work closely with his friend Paul Rotha, the director of documentary. He died of cancer in 1944.

Two films which were significant for recording the depression of the difficult years 1929 to 1932 were *Mother Krause's Journey to Happiness* (*Mutter Krauses Fahrt ins Gluck*, 1929), based on drawings by the artist, Heinrich Zille, and *Berlin-Alexanderplatz* (1931), adapted from Alfred Döblin's novel. These were directed by Piel (Phil) Jutzi, a cameraman turned director. The first was set in the Berlin slums familiar from Zille's drawings, which had already inspired a silent film made by Gerhard Lamprecht, *Slums of Berlin* (*Die Verrufenen*, 1925). The journey to happiness taken by Mother Krause is suicide after her daughter has been seduced and her son has been arrested for theft. In *Berlin-Alexanderplatz*, however, Jutzi allows his hero, a criminal and murderer played by Heinrich George, to end up an honest man. Nothing pays, not even crime. Jutzi's films are utterly fatalistic. Gerhard Lamprecht, however, also made the charming semi-documentary film, *Emil and the Detectives* (*Emil und die Detektive*, 1931), based on a best-selling novel by Erich Kästner, a film about a boy who is robbed of some money on his way by train to Berlin. A gang of boys come to his aid in pursuit of the thief, played with stylized stiffness by Fritz Rasp, a creature of darkness and shadow who is chased out into the sunlight as the children close in for the capture. This film, shot in a free style on location, is fresh, vigorous and human.

Fritz Lang's first sound film, *M* (1931), was to prove one of his finest, though the script was by Thea von Harbou. Lang told Kracauer that when the story of the Düsseldorf child-murders was first launched as an idea under the title *Murderers Amongst Us*, the studios he had hired were suddenly withdrawn by a studio manager whom Lang saw wearing the badge of the National Socialist Party. He had not realized what the film was about, and, unprompted, had thought it might be some form of attack upon Hitler! The film was magnificently handled technically, showing that the additional dimension of sound brought a new maturity to Lang's imagination. The murderer, brilliantly played as a fat, timorous man by Peter Lorre,[4] is eventually hauled before a 'court' formed by the underworld itself—because the criminals of Düsseldorf are as much against him and the disturbance and fear he creates as are the police. This was to be the beginning of Peter Lorre's international career as an actor.

It is interesting to compare this film with a lesser one which also deals with murder, the Russian Fedor Ozep's [5] German film *Karamasoff* (*Der Mörder Dimitri Karamasoff*, 1931), adapted from Dostoevsky, in which Karamasoff is wrongly suspected of the murder of his father which he has wanted to commit, though he has not had the courage to do so. The father's death is brought about by an epileptic servant. This is a well made film, but neither the level of acting nor the use of sound has anything of the imaginative power which Lang brought to *M*.

In 1931 Pabst made *The Threepenny Opera* (*Die Dreigroschenoper*), derived from Brecht's and Kurt Weill's play with songs, re-setting Gay's eighteenth-century play, *The Beggar's Opera*, in the late nineteenth century. The presentation of this stylized underworld was totally different from the realistic style which Pabst adopted in *Westfront 1918* and *Kameradschaft*. We are back in an underworld like that of *Pandora's Box*, a special world of light and shadow in which Pabst sought to combine his cinema of the 1920s with Brecht's form of theatrical presentation. Brecht had originally produced his version of *The Threepenny Opera* in 1928 in the Berlin Theater am Schiffbauerdam, now once again the theatre of the Berliner Ensemble, the company formed by Brecht in East Berlin after the Second World War. The phenomenal success of the play led to the demand for it to be filmed.[6] The story of Brecht's relationship to the film has been told by his associate, John Hans Winge (*Sight and Sound*, Winter, 1956 – 57):

With all his respect for the secrets of film-making, Brecht had definite artistic theories about the production, ideas linked, as always, to his political convictions. The producers assured him that his demands would be met, but in the heat of filming these promises were largely forgotten. Angered to discover that elementary parts of his message had been disregarded or eliminated, Brecht sued the company.

Pabst's film was of course a success, though on a rather less devastating scale than the stage production. Andreiev's excellent and original decors, Fritz Arno Wagner's camera-work, and the playing of a cast which included such members of the original company as Carola Neher (Polly Peachum) and Lotte Lenya (Weill's wife, who played the part of Jenny again in the recent New York stage production) were all highly and deservedly praised. But the film lacked the particular edge and sharpness of Brecht's wit and generally stressed the play's more romantic elements. It was shot in two versions, Macheath being played in the German version by the Austrian actor Rudolf Forster (on the stage by the springy and almost acrobatic Harald Paulsen) and in the French version by Albert Préjean.

Pabst had worked with Brecht himself on the script in the south of France during the summer of 1930, and their disagreement had begun at that time.

Arnold Fanck, as we have seen, specialized in outdoor subjects. He continued his mountaineering films into the era of sound with Leni Riefenstahl as his heroine. *Avalanche* (*Sturm über dem Montblanc*, 1930) was followed by *The White Frenzy* (*Der Weisse Rausch*, 1931), all clouds, mountainscapes, storms, ski-ing and rescue-work. Luis Trenker, one of Fanck's hero-stars, took the mythology of the mountains further in *Rebel* (*Der Rebell*, 1932), released a fortnight before Hitler came to power. Both are set in the Austrian Tyrol. In the first, Trenker, as a war hero, saves a battalion isolated on a mountain top from destruction by an Italian unit who are preparing to mine their position. The second concerns Tyrolean resistance during the Napoleonic Wars; it had Vilma Banky as the heroine, and Sepp Allgeier as cameraman—later to be Leni Riefenstahl's principal cameraman for *Triumph of the Will*, a film which opens, as we shall see, with massive cloudscapes set to music and an identification of Hitler as a man who descends like a god from the clouds to meet his people.

Leni Riefenstahl [7] broke away from Fanck to make her own independent production, *The Blue Light* (*Das Blaue Licht*, 1932), with a script by Béla Balázs based on a legend from the Italian Dolomites where her film was to be shot. Young men are lured to their destruction by the mysterious blue light which shines on the peak of Mount Cristallo at full moon. The only person who knows the secret of the blue light is Junta, an outcast girl, played by Leni Riefenstahl, who is thought to be a witch. She alone knows the way up the mountain face to the cave of the crystals, but her secret is discovered by a young painter who is in love with her.

To save further young men from destroying themselves, the painter reveals the secret of the way up to the cave, and an expedition is organized to remove the fatal crystals. At the next full moon it is Junta who falls to her death; the blue light which is her guide has gone. *The Blue Light* is a film which is part mystical, part legendary, and to some extent it anticipates the mountain 'mystique' of Hitler and the Berghof.

Certain of the films produced during this initial period of the German sound cinema were historical productions with a nationalist, even a political, intention. The series of films about Frederick the Great continued, and films concerning Prussian defiance during the Napoleonic invasion of German territory. These included Carl Froelich's *Luise, Königin von Preussen* (1931), *Yorck* (1931), directed by Gustav Ucicky, in which Werner Krauss played the general Yorck who in the end has to defy the weak King Frederick William of Prussia and start the war of German liberation from the French in defiance of him—and *The Flute Concert of Sanssouci* (*Das Flöten-konzert von Sanssouci*, 1930), also directed by Ucicky, in which Otto Gebühr gave another of his almost annual impersonations of the King. These nationalist films constantly kept the idea of a unified Germany's defiance of her dictatorial neighbours before the public in a romanticized form, with Frederick the Great as the wise and all-seeing ruler.

During the same period there were films which tried to pull back from nationalism and its implications that Germany's destiny lay in another war of 'liberation'. Among these, for example, were Richard Oswald's *The Captain of Köpenick* (*Der Hauptmann von Köpenick*, 1931), with its quiet mockery of Prussian militarism and unquestioning worship of the uniform whoever was in it, and Max Ophüls's [8] screen version of Schnitzler's *Liebelei* (1933), in which the harshness of the military code of the duel, and the waste of life and love which it entailed, are exposed. In spite of its Viennese charm, the implication is firmly put over.

Stronger films than these were to reach the screen before Goebbels possessed the power to stop them. A stage director, Leontine Sagan, made *Girls in Uniform* (*Mädchen in Uniform*, 1931) under the supervision of Carl Froelich for an independent company, and in a stark, inescapable story exposed the toll authoritarianism could take in its effect on young and sensitive minds. The headmistress of a school for the daughters of officers in Potsdam advocates discipline and toughness; one member of her staff, Fräulein von Bernburg (played by Dorothea Wieck), opposes her, but is unhappily betrayed when one of the pupils to whom she has given particular much-needed sympathy and affection blurts out that she is in love with her. The headmistress orders the girl, Manuela, to be ostracized, and only when she attempts suicide does the tyrant learn her lesson. The film is scarcely subversive in its exposure of militarism; rather it seeks to demonstrate a lesson to those who administer too harshly the necessities of discipline. This is revealed in the final arguments advanced to Manuela by Fräulein von Bernburg, and it is this apparent desertion by the only friend she has which leads to the girl's attempt at suicide. The film, however, was widely acclaimed for its humanitarianism, both in Germany and abroad. Herta Thiele, who played Manuela, and Dorothea Wieck appeared in a subsequent film, *Anna and Elizabeth* (1933), directed by Frank Wysbar, in which they portrayed a somewhat different relationship.

In *Eight Girls in a Boat* (*Acht Mädels im Boot*, 1932), directed by Erich Waschneck, *Girls in Uniform* had a curious successor in which a pregnant schoolgirl, terrified alike at the prospects of an abortion and the anger of her father, has to draw on the Amazonian strength of a blonde athletics coach, Hanna, who, since she represents the future Nazi conception of strength through physical discipline, outfaces the girl's father. After *Girls in Uniform*, Leontine Sagan went to England to direct a film about Oxford undergraduates, *Men of Tomorrow*.

Two films set out vigorously to expose the false heroics of war, Pabst's *Westfront 1918* (1930), and Victor Trivas's *Hell on Earth* (*Niemandsland*, 1931). Both were openly pacifist, but *Hell on Earth* (or *War is Hell*, as it has been sometimes retitled) is something of a fantasy in that five men of different race and nationality are for a while isolated in a no-man's-land between the fighting fronts and create a community of brotherhood together from which they are removed only by the approach of the warring armies. Pabst's sense of actuality in *Westfront 1918* is absolute; this is a study of men in the German trenches during the last phase of the war and engaged

in the routines of the lull before action. They discover the disloca-
tion of life caused by war when they return on leave, and the horror
of mutilation and death when eventually the attack on the war
front is resumed. Pabst's realism, called at the time the 'new
objectivity', was in effect an anticipation of neo-realism, though
much of it was achieved in the studio. Nothing on the battlefront
is picturesque or smokily beautiful; the total effect is grey and
neutral. The setting narrows down the representation of actuality,
selecting what is shown in order to present a significant, pictorial
realism of the kind associated with newsreels and documentaries
of war, yet achieved artificially. As Kracauer says:

Many shots betray the unconscious cruelty of the candid camera.
Helmets and fragments of corpses form a weird still life; somewhere
behind the front lines, several privates carry scores of wooden
crosses destined to adorn soldier graves. As always, Pabst manages
to avoid cheap symbolism. The undamaged statue of Christ in the
ruined church is made to appear a casual fact which only incidentally conveys a symbolic meaning. Throughout the film war seems
experienced rather than staged. To deepen this experience much
use is made of travelling shots. They are produced by a camera
which may travel long distances to capture the whole of some
scenery or action.

But Kracauer criticizes Pabst for thinking that the mere display
of the horrors of war would in itself be sufficient to deter society
from waging it. Perhaps conscious of this, Pabst altered the end
title to 'The End?'.

It is perhaps of interest that the art director both for this film
and *Kameradschaft* was the Hungarian, Ernö Metzner, director of
Accident; the cameraman was Fritz Arno Wagner. Wagner used
blimped mobile cameras in a period when cameras were still secured
in booths in the studios in order to keep their sound clear of the
microphone. The sets were lit very dimly to avoid any touch of
brightness. Luft, in his article on Pabst in *Films and Filming*, April
1967, describes the problem of controlling the sound:

No music was added to sustain the monotony. Since re-recording
was unknown in Germany at that time, sound effects had to be
mixed with the dialogue on the stage. When it became necessary
to add battle noise, the optical sound track of the negative had to

be undercut with small bits of effects to create artificially the illusion of machine gun fire, shrapnel shots and the thunder of big guns—without re-dubbing.

Comradeship (*Kameradschaft*, 1931) remains one of Pabst's finest films. Based on an actual episode which took place before the First World War, when German miners went to assist in the rescue of French miners just over the border after a disaster at Courrières, Pabst brought his reconstruction of a similar event to the period immediately following the Versailles Treaty. Roger Manvell has written elsewhere of this film:

But the authenticity goes beyond the effective use of locations or the scientifically accurate reconstruction of the disaster below-ground; it extends to the characters themselves. None of them, German or French, is given special prominence. They receive just sufficient portrayal to establish themselves as decent people of a kind likely to be working in these mining communities on either side of the Franco-German frontier. The pathos of the old French grandfather, an ex-miner whose grandson is involved in the disaster on his first day below-ground, is not the pathos of an actor working up an emotional role. His suffering is an extension of the anxiety of a whole community, a channel through which Pabst is able to express the intense feeling of all the relatives of the trapped and dying men. Similarly, there is a touching scene in which a woman with a worn and sunken face runs beside the slowly moving lorry which is carrying her German husband off as a member of the volunteer rescue expedition going over the border. She holds on to her child, the symbol of her link to this man who may not come back. It is like a parting before war, a parting which belongs to the life of a community that must inevitably work and struggle.

The technique developed by Pabst derives in part from the Russian silent documentary films which he had seen, but whereas the outstanding Soviet directors of the twenties adopted certain forms of stylization to offset the realism of their subjects (as, for example, in *Potemkin* or in *The Ghost that Never Returns*), Pabst aims directly at realistic effect. The famous brief episode of hallucination, when a trapped French miner hysterical with fear sees his masked German rescuer as if he were still an enemy on the battlefront, is obviously the kind of fantasy which arises naturally out of psychological realism. But Pabst shows himself to be a film-maker of depth and imagination in the way he uses the technical capacities of the new sound-film to dramatize the key situations in this story of disaster and human courage. It is this capacity of his to dramatize these situations without any loss of realistic atmosphere which gives his film a power that the years do not diminish.

There are many examples of this imaginative handling of people and situations in the film—the scenes inside the mine immediately following the explosions, the gradual enlargement of the running crowd of people summoned by the alarm from the pithead, the crowd scenes at the gates when the waiting women, at first so desperate and demanding, eventually break up into passively waiting groups, sitting where they can as they face the inevitable hours while the search goes on for the bodies of their men, living and dead. With a cunning montage of shots involving static cameras gathering telling details and tracking cameras identified with the running crowd, while the sound track represents the ebb and flow of human cries and the clatter of running feet, Pabst builds up a sympathetic identification between the mining community and the audience which is to watch their suffering. Working in the early, exciting days of sound, Pabst had the imagination often to impose complete silence on a scene. Often, too, he makes prolonged use of the simplest kind of natural sound, like the moaning roar which comes up from the mine-shaft when the old man climbs down to find Georges, his grandson, or the intense pulsation of an artificial respirator, or the simple echo of the old man's voice in the cavernous emptiness of the mine as he cries 'Georges ... Georges ...', an echo which emphasizes like music the piteous anxiety of his search, or the gradually quickening rhythm of the alternate tappings when the three trapped Germans are discovered by the rescuers, and finally burst into peal after peal of hysterically happy laughter when they know that they are safe. This continuous close sympathy of Pabst with the dramatic content of the situations he is handling on the screen is the result of a sensitive artistic imagination, just as his recognition of the pictorial value of including, for example, the fantastic yet realistic scene of the German miners' bath hall, with its foliage of clothes slung on chains high above the naked man, adds at the same time a fine element of authenticity to the background of life in a mining community. Indeed every important shot is composed with care, so that the realistic qualities of the film are always served by an artist's eye for the formal beauties.

This was the last considerable film to be made by Pabst. Disillusioned by the lack of support his film received in Germany, where it was attacked in the reactionary press and played to empty seats even in working-class areas, Pabst retired to Paris, where the film, in a less radical French version, enjoyed some success. It won a prize awarded by the League of Nations. Pabst was not to make another film in Germany until his controversial return to Hitler's Reich in 1939. This was significant in the light of an interview he gave in Belgium in 1933 after making *Don Quixote* in France:

'*Pandora's Box* . . . *Crisis* . . . *The Diary of a Lost Girl* . . . have undergone all sorts of censuring. *Westfront 1918* because of its pacific character, was the object of the lowest kind of manœuvres. I am the most attacked director in Europe and I pay dearly for my independence. After *L'Atlantide* I waited months and months for a proposition which I could accept without caving in. That's where candour leads you. In Hollywood, von Stroheim has lost his last supports. The set-back—supposed—of *Walking Down Broadway* was sufficient for the backers to withdraw their confidence from one of the greatest craftsmen of the cinema. King Vidor only signed *Street Scene* to get his name on *Bird of Paradise*. As regards Sternberg, I met him in Paris hardly twenty-four hours ago. In America all doors are closed to him. He came to Europe to try to find work. Everybody in France as well as Germany drew back. He leaves again to-night for the States. What will he do there?'

A silence. Then:

'I don't reproach business men for gaining money, or for the desire to earn it. I dream of an understanding between the audience and the director, apart from the production. To appreciate each other they must understand one another. That is why I like to have meetings with cinema journalists in different countries.'

'Do you foresee a reorganization of production?'

'Rather the creation of another production better adapted to the needs of those for whom it will be intended.'

'Perhaps in collaboration with the state?'

'No! Hitler today and Stalin tomorrow! Under an obligation to direct oneself according to the wish of each Government. Never! There must be freedom to follow a determined line once and for all.'

. . . .

'A film must take a side.

'The cinema is the mirror of our epoch in which everything must be reflected and imprinted for ever.' [9]

Brecht's disillusionment with Pabst did not take so negative a form. The year after the split between them over *The Threepenny Opera*, Brecht worked with Ernst Ottwald on the script of *Kuhle Wampe* (1932). The title of the film is the name given to the colony of the unemployed who lived in tents outside Berlin at that time.

It was directed by a young Bulgarian, Slatan Dudow, and was a film with a distinct left-wing tendency. The story concerns a disillusioned working-class family in which only the daughter, Anni (Herta Thiele) has a job; the father resorts to drink, the son to suicide. Thrown out of their tenement lodging, the family is forced to go to Kuhle Wampe. Anni is pregnant, but rejects her lover when he is reluctant to marry her and urges her to have an abortion. She leaves the whole reactionary working-class world her parents represent and joins a left-wing workers' sports club where she can enjoy healthier companionship. The film ends on a positive note, and Anni is reconciled to her lover. But the film implies that only the young among the workers can be forward-looking and, in the words of the theme-song, 'determine to alter and better the world'. The censors objected to *Kuhle Wampe*, and it was released only after a number of cuts had been made. The film was produced under the greatest difficulties and, it would seem, was only completed at all through the pertinacity of Dudow, who did not make another film in Germany until after the war, and then in the East. The male lead was played by Ernst Busch, famous in Berlin for his revolutionary songs; he had also played the ballad-singer in *The Threepenny Opera*, and a leading part in *Kameradschaft*. He left Germany to join the International Brigade in Spain, and he was later imprisoned by the Nazis. After the war he joined Brecht's Berliner Ensemble. Brecht himself had to leave after Hitler came to power; he finally went to Hollywood, where he worked with Lang on the script of *Hangmen also Die*, which dealt with the assassination of Heydrich in Prague during the war. It is of interest to note that the same situation arose in his relations with Lang as in the case of Pabst; Brecht disagreed strongly over the slant to be given his work by the technical script-writers and Lang in Hollywood.

The film which, according to its maker, set out to challenge Hitler in the form of an allegory was never shown in Germany. This was Fritz Lang's *The Last Will of Dr Mabuse* (*Das Testament des Dr Mabuse*, 1933) finished in 1932 just before Hitler came to power in January 1933. It was banned by Goebbels, as Minister for Propaganda, before it could be released. The French version, however, was edited later in France, which prevented the film from being destroyed. The mad doctor of Lang's earlier film was revived for this thriller; in his lunatic asylum he plans all the details for the destruction of mankind. He gains an hypnotic hold over Dr Baum, his psychiatrist, who under his influence forms a movement in the criminal underworld to carry out his designs. When Mabuse dies, Baum believes himself to be the madman's reincarnated self. He is finally defeated by the same detective who discovered the murderer in *M*, the highly rational Chief Inspector Lohmann.

Fritz Lang subsequently claimed that he had Hitler in mind when making this film. He told the authors, as he told others, that this was so, and that Goebbels banned it for this reason. Goebbels's ban at least bears out the claim, though when the film is seen today it appears very doubtful whether the German public would have grasped the parallel intended in this brilliantly made fantasy.[10]

Chapter four

The film in Nazi
Germany – i

To understand something of what happened to the film industry, and especially to production under the Nazis, it is necessary to understand the nature of the régime itself and its attitude to the propaganda which was designed to sustain and increase its power. The rule of Hitler, which lasted twelve years and led to the death of over fifty million people during the climactic years of war and genocide, was ultimately a personal act of revenge, aggression and conquest. In Germany, and later in the German-occupied countries also, it was absolute rule by a single Party, the National Socialist German Labour Party, the N.S.D.A.P. (*Nationalsozialistische Deutsche Arbeiter Partei*), which outlawed all others and maintained its tyranny by establishing a police state through the secret political police of the S.S. (*Schutzstaffel*), the Blackshirts, and the security police, the Gestapo (*Geheime Staatspolizei*). The sanctions for non-conformity to Hitler's will were the Gestapo's prisons and the concentration camps of the S.S., which during the war developed organized slave labour on a mass scale, and in certain specialized places, primarily in occupied Poland, centres for mass extermination. Hitler, who in 1925 was nothing but an able agitator recently released from confinement, was within fifteen years to be master of a greater empire than Napoleon ever ruled, stretching from Norway to the Mediterranean, and from the Atlantic coast to the outskirts of Leningrad and Moscow.

A régime as ruthless by effect as Hitler's could not exist without the constant application of propaganda on the minds of his people. Propaganda was defined by Hitler himself in *Mein Kampf*, which he wrote while in confinement in 1924:

The art of propaganda consists precisely in being able to awaken the imagination of the public through an appeal to their feelings, in finding the appropriate psychological form that will arrest the attention and appeal to the hearts of the national masses. . . .

The receptive powers of the masses are very restricted, and their understanding is feeble. On the other hand, they quickly forget. Such being the case, all effective propaganda must be confined to a few bare essentials and those must be expressed as far as possible in stereotyped formulae. These slogans should be persistently repeated until the very last individual has come to grasp the idea that has been put forward. . . .

Propaganda must not investigate the truth objectively and, in so far as it is favourable to the other side, present it according to the theoretical rules of justice; but it must present only that aspect of the truth which is favourable to its own side. . . .

As soon as our own propaganda makes the slightest suggestion that the enemy has a certain amount of justice on his side, then we lay down the basis on which the justice of our own cause could be questioned.

Propaganda, therefore, is the attempt to confine men's minds to a single line of thought which leads them to take action in support of the propagandists. It must exclude rational arguments, or any form of dangerous reasoning which might prejudice the propagandist's case. If propaganda is to be totally effective, it can exist only in a mental vacuum within which every other form of expression, political or religious, educational or artistic, is equally enclosed. The nonconformist must simply disappear, while every kind of expression which continues to function in the police state, such as the schools and universities, the churches and centres of entertainment, the press and publishing, must either adopt the ideology thrust upon them, or function solely as purveyors of innocuous 'escape', which offers no threat whatsoever to the Party line. The Nazis had a word for it—*Gleichschaltung*, putting everything into the same gear.

This was the policy imposed from 1933 by Dr Joseph Goebbels, Hitler's celebrated campaign manager during the crucial series of elections which finally brought Hitler to absolute power by May 1933, when the Enabling Act was passed which made him dictator. All forms of public expression—the press, radio, film, theatre, music, light entertainment, cabaret, and even the circus—came under Goebbels's jurisdiction, through the Ministry of Propaganda and Public Enlightenment established immediately after Hitler became Chancellor, but given legal entity on 13th March 1933.[1]

Prior to 1933 the Nazis had naturally exercised what influence they could on the press, radio and film. In 1927 Alfred Hugenberg, then Chairman of Krupp, had, as we have seen, bought up UFA. In 1928 he became Chairman of the German National Party, which had views similar to those of Hitler. After this his UFA staff, especially in their newsreels, showed a marked nationalist outlook. Hugenberg also controlled Deulig, whose newsreels—*Wochenschau*, and later, with the coming of sound, *Tonwoche* (issued with sound only in January 1932)—were equally nationalist in outlook. UFA controlled some four-fifths of German newsreel production and held a dominant position in screening through UFA cinemas and independent cinemas with UFA distribution contracts. The powerful film production and exhibition complex represented by the combination of UFA and Deulig presented a ready-made nationalist organization for Goebbels to take over in 1933.

Goebbels had already acquired some experience of the potentialities of the film before 1933. For example, Party rallies had been increasingly covered by Hugenberg's newsreel crews; the rallies made news. Thus the Party struggle, especially with the Communists, who produced newsreel and documentaries for use at their own party meetings, extended to the screen. Goebbels also produced his own election campaign film, shown by means of mobile projection equipment, sometimes in the open air. A film section was formed in the Party propaganda office with instructions which were not confined to production, but prepared the ground for a nation-wide organization for the take-over of the industry once the Party was in power, even to the extent of establishing the first stages of a regional organization for the production and screening of Party films. The organizers in charge of these regional areas were later to be placed in key positions in Goebbels's administration in 1933. The early films showed Hitler and Goebbels speaking at rallies similar to those at which they would be shown, together with the spectacle of the Storm Troopers' parades. Others took on a more 'documentary' form, with such titles as *Der Kampf um Berlin* or *Hitlers Flug über Deutschland*. These Party films, small in number at first, were backed by a far greater output of Party newsprint. Though officially banned other than for private screening, there was little actual interference with their showing to general audiences, especially in the villages. With the economic difficulties attendant on the coming of sound, many of the smaller cinemas were only too happy to keep just inside the margin of business by helping the Nazis, who in turn helped them by supporting programmes which included Nazi shorts, or by hiring their cinemas for the so-called private shows. The lax censorship laws made interference with Nazi screenings, protected as they were by strong-arm thugs of the S.A., far less likely than was the case in the Communist films, the ideology of which was recognized as subversive.

The Party film section published its own journal from 1932, *Der Deutsche Film*, and the attack on the Jews in the German film industry began in earnest. Statistics were published which purported to expose an overwhelming Jewish influence in production —claiming, for example, that forty per cent of the scripts of the year's feature films were written by Jews, and that eighty-six per cent of current production came from Jewish-owned companies, representing seventy per cent of the production companies in existence; this was a gross exaggeration of the admitted prominence of Jewish artists and executives in the industry. Another function of the film section was to set up disturbances and cause violence at the screening of films of which the Party did not approve, such as *All Quiet on the Western Front*, the American film adapted from Remarque's pacifist novel about the First World War, and the left-wing film *Kuhle Wampe*.

Goebbels, therefore, was well placed to take control of an industry which was already partly prepared to be controlled. Nevertheless, in a large and complex state like Germany, which had practised great freedom and even licence in artistic expression over an extended period of time, and especially during the 1920s, the new controls could scarcely be established overnight. Goebbels, it must be remembered, was not only a skilful agitator and public speaker; he was an able and ruthless administrator and a propagandist with a skill and intuitive judgment which were little short of genius. He did not make the same mistake as the Communist propagandists in the Soviet Union under Stalin, by imposing too great a burden of propaganda on the entertainment industries. He realized that even the most dedicated Nazis must have their lighter moments,

68

and relax with fun and games. He confined the solid grind of daily propaganda to the press, and let the entertainment industries, for the most part, simply entertain. With the important exception of newsreels and documentary films, only the so-called 'highlights', in the form of occasional 'prestige' feature films, gave full expression to Nazi ideology on the screen; the rest, the great majority of productions, were merely romantic dramas, comedies, musicals, and spectacular historical epics, films which represented, if they revealed anything at all, general entertainment, sometimes of a high standard.

To achieve this (from Goebbels's point of view) desirable condition a complex of laws, decrees and intricate state machinery was gradually created to stop up any loophole for nonconformity. Following a line which was to become traditional in the Hitler State, the Party organization was kept separate from State administration at both national and regional levels, but at the same time they became closely interlocked. This gave the mark of 'legality' and 'constitutional procedure' to what was soon to be the Party's control of all that mattered most in the functioning of the constitution, though nominally the State and the Party were differentiated. Thus, Goebbels's propaganda machine functioned as a Ministry, and was nominally distinct from the Party's propaganda machine, from which it directly sprang and which provided its key administrators immediately Hitler became Chancellor. The Ministry established its regional offices in the *Länder*, Germany's various administrative districts; the Party divided the nation into its own specifically political areas, or *Gaue*, under the Party Gauleiters, but the Ministry's regional offices corresponded to the *Gaue*, and the Ministry's chief propaganda officers at local level were the same as the Party's.

Goebbels exercised control through establishing an all-embracing system of *Reichskulturkammer*, or State Chambers of Culture, one for each main branch of expression—in Art, Music, Theatre, Authorship, Press, Radio, and Film. Goebbels acted as President of the Chambers of Culture, and through him their jurisdiction spread down to the administrative levels of *Land* and *Gau*. Thus the various departments of Goebbels's Ministry were directly linked with the appropriate Chambers of Culture, so that their directives could pass down the chain of command to those actually engaged in editing and journalism, drama and film production, writing and broadcasting, creating or exhibiting works of art, composing and performing music, whether serious or light, in concert-hall, music-hall or cabaret. A *Filmkammer* was set up provisionally in July 1933 to take over the administration of the film industry in all its branches, and was officially established as a section of the *Reichs-kulturkammer* when this was founded in September 1933.[2]

The *Reichsfilmkammer* exercised full control over what was produced and over whoever worked in the studios and in non-studio film-making—departments were set up to examine, in each professional and technical sector of the industry, their racial origin and political reliability. The professional and industrial organizations which already existed in the film industry were not necessarily disbanded—rather they were absorbed into the *Reichsfilmkammer*. Their retention at all was a kind of empty gesture from the State and Party; so was the nominal retention of individual film-producing companies. In any case, all workers in the industry had to become members of the *Deutsche Arbeitsfront*, the only official trade union.

Supervisory departments in the *Reichsfilmkammer* controlled each section of the industry, such as exhibition, distribution, and export, as well as the more specialist branches such as the cultural and educational film, tourist film, advertising film, and so forth. All this was carried through administratively from State to *Land* level. The Ministry, too, had departments for censorship, import of foreign films, film preservation, and control of film training at the school established in 1938 at Babelsberg,[3] and, most important, control of newsreels which centred on much direct production under Fritz Hippler after 1939. The controls were complete.

The effect of this on film production in particular is what we have to assess. The loss of talent, in particular Jewish talent, was naturally severe. From the moment Hitler came to power no Jew could be employed in any branch of the industry. Among the famous talents immediately lost to the theatre and films were: Gropius, Pölzig, Fritz and Adolph Busch, Carl Ebert, Max Reinhardt, Albert Bassermann, Lubitsch, Dieterle, Conrad Veidt, Lotte Lehmann, Liesl Bergner, Elsa Brandström, Lucie Mannheim, Berthold Viertel, Fritz Kortner, Oscar Homolka, Victor Barnowsky, Eugen Robert, Heinz Herald, Rudolf Forster, Marlene Dietrich, Richard Tauber,

Luise Rainer, Wolfgang Langhoff, Lilli Palmer, Vera Schwarz, Irene Eisinger, Ernst Deutsch, Eric Charell and many others.

Among the writers who had to leave Germany were: Thomas and Heinrich Mann, Lion Feuchtwanger, Stephan and Arnold Zweig, Bert Brecht, Georg Kaiser, Robert Musil, Leonard Frank, Carl Zuckmayer, Robert Neumann, Franz Werfel, Alfred Polgar, Oscar-Maria Graf, Erich Maria Remarque, Ludwig Renn, Alfred Kerr, Vicky Baum, Alfred Neumann, Stefan Lorant, Egon Erwin Kisch, Richard Lewinsohn, Alfred Döblin, Friedrich Wolff, Walter Mehring, Rom Landau, Siegfried Trebitsch, and Felix Salten.

However, the Nazis retained the services of many talented and skilful artists and technicians, such as Werner Krauss, Gustav Ucicky, Veit Harlan, Heinrich George, Hans Albers,[4] Otto Gebühr, Paul Wegener, Willy Fritsch, and, eventually, Emil Jannings and even G. W. Pabst.

Official control of production took many forms—establishing a *Filmkreditbank* in June 1933 to make loans to producers, so that production could get under way again after the recession which followed the upheavals caused by the arrival of the new régime; establishing a monopoly in sound-film equipment; establishing a firm censorship by the Reich Film Law of February 1934, which meant that scripts were scrutinized before production, and changes enforced; establishing a system of awarding 'marks of distinction' for films deemed worthy either politically or culturally, which in the case of films shown in public cinemas meant substantial entertainment tax deductions. All these interventions, from censorship to the assessment of political worthiness, were represented in a positive light—to establish the 'healthiness' of films and their high cultural quality, for the same reasons as nonconformists were imprisoned and Jews expelled. Old films of merit were soon banned on the grounds of the 'ill-health' they spread around—*Westfront 1918* and *Kameradschaft*, *Mädchen in Uniform* and *M*, even *Congress Dances* —on the grounds, like those affecting *M*, that Jews had participated prominently in their production. Film criticism, once on a high level in Germany, sank into a mere journalistic record of political acceptibility. Goebbels even went so far as to issue an edict that all criticism must be 'positive'.

The effect of these controls was to lower the temperature of

German film-making until it approached zero, except for such enthusiastic propaganda films as Leni Riefenstahl's *Triumph of the Will*. German films became escapist and politically harmless, or nondescript; and notable for the absence, rather than the presence, of a swastika. They were technically impeccable, earning good marks for art and not for propaganda. Average production costs rose, more than quadrupled in fact, between 1933 and the final nationalization of the industry in 1942; they had more than doubled by 1939. Public support of the cinema slackened until the war years, when it recovered; many films lost money. Under the supervision of their economic adviser, Dr Max Winkler, the State planned the acquisition of the sinking film industry during 1941; it was a process which had been going on quietly underground since UFA had been acquired in 1937 by the regular Nazi practice of driving firms out of business, and then taking them over at nominal rates by some combine under their control. The 'independent' film companies went down like ninepins. In a similar way, the exhibition branch of the industry became increasingly standardized, ownership was amalgamated and taken over, and the professions of manager and projectionist were controlled. The number of cinemas remained around 5,000, but with quality of projection greatly improved; audiences, however, averaged only some 40 per cent of capacity until wartime suddenly inflated the attraction of cinema-going.[5] An increasing ratio of German films was shown, as compared with importations: 42 per cent in 1935, 79 per cent in 1939. German production stood at an average level of about one hundred features a year, and dropped to as low as sixty before nationalization in 1942. At the same time, German films found new, compulsory outlets in the occupied countries. At home the highest proportion of films shown were comedies, the smallest those with some direct kind of political content. In the occupied countries, propaganda newsreels playing as long as one hour were common, and subtitled German features were the most prominent import, even in countries such as France, where a strong pre-war industry was to some extent being maintained under the strict control of the occupation authorities.

The Party film organization was also maintained—its function to promote the propaganda film in schools and for the Hitler Youth.

In 1935, for example, 141 national and 160 local films were made, and over 121,000 screenings with mobile equipment organized; a total staff of 25,000, paid and voluntary, took part at all levels. Most of the school films were silent shorts, but large-scale shows using 35-mm. projectors were frequent, with mass open-air screenings at rallies. Special Party film festivals and folk film days showed the extent to which the Party came to depend on films both before and during the war.

It can be seen, therefore, that Goebbels placed a high priority on the film both as a medium for propaganda and as escapist entertainment. On 28 March 1933, only two months after Hitler became Chancellor, he called a representative body of film-makers and film journalists together at the Kaiserhof. He spoke about the attitude of the régime to films and the industry which produced them. Films, he said, were to have an important place in the culture of the new Germany; he was clever enough to make the future look very rosy for those who wanted to make good films. He surprised his audience by praising Eisenstein's film *The Battleship Potemkin* as well as Lang's *Nibelung Saga*. Nothing reflects better the cynical opportunism with which Goebbels exercised his authority while the Nazis were still at the height of their power than the frequent allusions to the cinema in certain of his private wartime diaries which have survived:

Film production is flourishing almost unbelievably despite the war. What a good idea of mine it was to have taken possession of the films on behalf of the Reich several years ago! It would be terrible if the high profits now being earned by the motion-picture industry were to flow into private hands. . . .

All motion-picture producers visited me. In the evening we see the American Technicolor picture *Swanee River*, which affords me an opportunity for making a number of observations on the creation of a new German film based on folk songs. The fact of the matter is that the Americans have the ability of taking their relatively small stock of culture and by a modernized version to make of it something that is very *a propos* for the present time. We are loaded down altogether too much with tradition and piety. We hesitate to clothe our cultural heritage in a modern dress. It therefore remains purely historical or museum-like and is at best understood by groups within the Party, the Hitler Youth, or the Labour Service.

The cultural heritage of our past can be rendered fruitful for the present on a large scale only if we present it with modern means. The Americans are masters at this sort of thing, I suppose, because they are not weighed down as much as we are with political ballast. Nevertheless we shall have to do something about it. The Americans have only a few Negro songs, but they present them in such a modern way that they conquer large parts of the modern world which is, of course, very fond of such melodies. We have a much greater fund of cultural goods, but we have neither the artistry nor the will to modernize them. That will have to be changed. . . .

I ordered Greven to come to Berlin from Paris, to give him absolutely clear and unmistakable directions to the effect that for the moment, so far as the French are concerned, only light and frothy, and, if possible, corny pictures are desired. No doubt the French people will be satisfied with that too. There is no reason why we should cultivate their nationalism.

All actors of more than average talent in the French movies should, as far as possible, be hired by us for German film production. . . .

Germany was in the strait-jacket. What films did they make?

Chapter five

The film in Nazi
Germany – ii

It must be emphasized again that the bulk of the feature films produced during the twelve-year period of the Nazi régime, numbering in fact some 1,100, were of a purely escapist nature, containing little or no political references or even undertones. This was Goebbels's deliberate policy in order to fill the cinemas, where the supporting section of the programme, the newsreels and documentaries, carried the current Nazi message. But in the majority of the feature films not a swastika was to be seen; they were competently made, though with few exceptions 'empty' as far as real human values were concerned. Most of those films, numbering, it would seem, around fifty, which did have a specifically nationalist or, more narrowly, National Socialist statement in their conception or action were also well made, but also relatively 'empty' from the human and psychological point of view. The characters stood for their statements rather than for themselves. But among the specifically Nazi films there were included a few which, in spite of their negative human values, were nevertheless outstanding in their kind. Among these were Leni Riefenstahl's *Triumph of the Will* (*Triumph des Willens*, 1935),[1] a lyrical paean of praise of Hitler belonging to the early 'honeymoon' period of Nazism when a majority of the German people were in love with Hitler; and later, during the war, such contentious films as *Baptism of Fire*, *Victory in the West*, Hans Steinhoff's *Ohm Krüger* (1941) and, above all, *The Eternal Jew* (*Der Ewige Jude*, 1940), Franz Hippler's virulent anti-Semitic film, the most vicious piece of propaganda of its kind to be made by the Nazis, but nevertheless a 'black masterpiece' as a demonstration of how the medium can be 'bent' in the service of a vile cause.

Films with some specifically Nazi theme, or with a strongly nationalist emphasis of the kind most advocated by the National

Socialist platform, can be considered in various categories.[2] First come the initial propaganda films, including feature-length documentaries, advocating the Party, the Third Reich and, above all, the Führer. In 1933, for example, there was *Hans Westmar*, directed by Franz Wenzler, which purported to be a biography of Horst Wessel, presenting him as a Nazi martyr killed by the Communists. The funeral procession, in itself a provocative demonstration, is shown in an emotional climax. Horst Wessel, in fact, was little better than a pimp, a Nazi street-fighter who died in a brawl with another man, Ali Hoehler, who was also a pimp. But he had written the words eventually set to hymn-like music purloined from the Communists, which became the Nazi anthem, the *Horst Wessel Lied*. Also in 1933 there was Franz Seitz's *S.A. Mann Brand*, which tells the story of a young Nazi who leaves home because his father is a Communist, and is subsequently murdered by the Communists. This, however, only serves to increase Party fanaticism at the ensuing elections; the boy is another martyr to the cause. Hans Steinhoff's *Hitlerjunge Quex*, which also featured the Nazi son of a Communist father and starred Heinrich George, appeared in the same year. The boy betrays a Communist plan to wreck a Hitler Youth hostel; his mother, fearful of vengeance at the hands of the Communists, commits suicide, while the boy himself, like Horst Wessel, is murdered at election time. The flag stained with his blood is adopted by the National Socialists after the election is won. The following year, 1934, Carl Froelich produced and directed *Ich für Dich—Du für mich*, a story of duty to others, and above all to the Fatherland, set in a Women's Labour Corps Camp in Germany.

An interesting documentary film made in 1936 by Hans Springer presents the Nazi nationalist and racial mythology in a poetic, or pseudo-poetic, form. This is *The Eternal Forest* (*Ewiger Wald*) a one-hour film with continuous music by Wolfgang Zeller, often with choral backing. It springs from the tradition of the typical soft-centred, photographically impeccable 'Kulturfilm', and its commentary, conceived in a kind of doggerel verse, is spoken in deep, portentous tones. The film opens with a long sequence of beautiful forest scenes, passing through the seasons, from winter to spring, presented with lyrical, choral effects. Then a caption announces that the Reich is imperishable, like the forest.

The film traces the history of the German people back to early times of settlement and development of the sacred soil. Their dances are pagan. 'God is silent', cries the voice. 'But still we may rest under his sun.' When the Romans with their eagle-standards come to threaten the peace of this countryside, the people, sensing their mortal danger, fight for their existence. The sequence ends with a funeral pyre. Then, presented as a prolonged montage lasting several minutes, we follow the German people through the age of the coming of Christianity, the age of the troubadour, of the Crusades, to the period of the Teutonic knights. This leads to scenes of the forge and the cutting of timber, while the commentator declaims about 'the glory and power of German cities built with wood'. 'German faces' and 'German hands' are seen in works of art, in statues, in churches and cathedrals. A slow pan up a Gothic cathedral spire dissolves into the spire of a tree.

A sequence of the Peasant War of the sixteenth century shows the demand of the German people for recognition. 'What the Church once took, she keeps', says the voice. 'For every tree, a peasant should rise too.' A complete reel of ten minutes is devoted to the peasant uprising, followed by the devastation of the Thirty Years' War. 'The peasant is dead; the people are in need; the fields are deserted.' But under Frederick the Great all is restored. 'The King wants new forests to stand up like soldiers.'

The transition to modern times is achieved by an impressionistic sequence of German nineteenth-century romantic painting, via Strauss to the twentieth century, and the felling of trees to symbolize the devastation of the First World War, during which the soldiers sing *Heilige Nacht* in the trenches. The end of the war is represented by a panorama of graves, the occupation of the Ruhr by coloured soldiers (presumably Algerians) supervising the felling of further trees, and the transportation of logs in chains, presumably in reparation to France. 'How can you bear this suffering, my folk, my forests?' cries the voice. The answer comes with a new forest, that of a massed panorama of Nazi flags, adorned with their swastikas. The early pagan rites are recalled, linking the end to the beginning. Peasants dance round the Maypole in pagan ritual. The forests stand again, along with the ranks of the Nazis. The film reflects, in lyrical form, the familiar Nazi 'philosophy' that the pure German race is essentially a peasant aristocracy, a racial *Herrenvolk* whose roots lie in the soil fertilized for centuries by the riches of their blood.

In the category of the early propaganda film, there is nothing to equal the mastery of Leni Riefenstahl's *Triumph of the Will* (1936). This film celebrated the significance of Hitler's leadership of the German people as symbolized in the annual Party Congress at Nuremberg in September 1934, the greatest gathering of its kind, involving a million and a half people. Thirty cameramen and a large technical staff were assembled to make the film; pits were dug before the speakers' rostrum; tracks for travelling shots and lifts for panoramic shots taken from a height were constructed. Hitler, who was an enthusiast for Leni Riefenstahl's work in the cinema, had commissioned her to undertake the film without any proper understanding with Goebbels in the matter, an action quite typical of the Führer. Goebbels was, understandably, very angry, and was determined to sabotage the film by such means as lay open to him—which, in the circumstances of the Führer's will in the matter, meant making the physical conditions governing the film coverage of the Congress as difficult as possible. For Leni Riefenstahl, on the other hand, this was the opportunity of a lifetime, and she gave the film every ounce of her energy and talent; she lifts what would have been a dreary parade of rhetoric, marches, and mass spectacle into an evocation of what Hitler meant to her personally and to the German people, and it is this emotionalism which is conveyed through the whole tempo of the film, with its rhythmic cutting, its carefully contrived sequences binding the ancient traditions of Germany (seen in the architecture of Nuremberg, for example) with the near-deification of Hitler as he is received by the assembled masses of his supporters. The film was eventually premiered in the UFA-Palast cinema, receiving a State prize, the Gold Medal at the Venice Film Festival of 1935, and a Grand Prix awarded by the French Government at the Paris film festival.[3] Since this film has so special an interest, we include a full outline of its treatment:

Prolonged orchestral play-in, Wagnerian style. Slow fade-up, of the German eagle, and the title 'TRIUMPH DES WILLENS', and the caption:
'Made by order of the Führer 20 years since the outbreak of the

World War, 16 years after the beginning of the German misery, 19 months after the beginning of the German Renaissance: 1934, the Party Congress.'

The Führer approaches through the clouds, his plane weaving through the white masses. The music is soft and romantic, the effect godlike. Nuremberg appears below. The Horst Wessel Nazi anthem starts. The shadow of Hitler's plane passes up a long line of marching men in the street below. Shot by shot, we descend nearer to the streets and the city full of marching columns.

The airport. The plane taxis in. The welcoming crowds crane forward, their arms a sea of Nazi salutes. The Leader emerges. The crowd surges with enthusiasm. Goebbels in a raincoat follows the Führer, grinning with pleasure.

The drive into Nuremberg. The camera is behind Hitler in the car, angled up, concentrating on his arm extended in salute. The crowds are lining the streets and saluting him. Montage of Hitler's arm and the crowds as the car drives along the endless streets thronged with people. The music builds, reflecting the emotion of welcome. Hitler's car stops for a mother and her little girl to present flowers to the Führer. During the journey there are frequent shots of people in the crowds, people at the windows above, even a cat on a beflagged balcony.

Nuremberg, its Gothic roofs, its medieval fountains, its Nazi flags. Hitler's face is now stiff and set, now as near smiling as he can be. Soldiers are shown with handsome faces turned sideways to the sun. Lines of jackboots. 'Sieg Heil,' the crowds shout. Hitler arrives, and stands out on the balcony above the crowds, smiling.

The first night of the Rally. Torches; martial music; bonfires. Pictorial effects with streams of smoke lit by floodlights. Silhouettes of helmeted heads. The transparent veils of the flags and banners lit from behind in the night.

Dawn over the roofs of Nuremberg. The great Rally camp for youth. Slow 'dawn' music accompanies the rousing of the sleepers. Camp scenes. Food. Wrestling matches. The laughing boys. Procession of men and girls in folk costume, parading in the streets of Nuremberg. A little girl gnaws an apple. Cut from the little girl to Hitler, the father of his people. He shakes hands with chosen young delegates in their folk costumes. Close-ups reveal Hitler's searching interest in what is going on. He talks to the representatives of the youth movement. A little boy presses his fingers in his mouth as he watches the Führer.

The Congress Hall filled with a vast perspective of people. Light floods onto their heads; onto the symbolic eagles. Hess speaks: 'We think of the dead. We greet our foreign guests. We see the revival of the Wehrmacht under the Führer. The greatness of the future; only then will the Führer be appreciated as he should be. The Führer is Germany; when he judges, the nation judges [reference to Roehm purge]. Germany is home for all Germans from all over the world.'

Wagnerian music. The leaders come forward to pay their tributes to Hitler. Rosenberg is sweating. Dietrich—'we want the truth to be presented about the German people.' Streicher wants to see racial purity. Goebbels: 'The flame of our enthusiasm gives life and warmth; it comes from the deep-down roots of our people. It is good to have guns and bayonets, but better to have the hearts of the nation.' Hitler is acclaimed.

Hitler addresses the Labour Force, who stand marshalled in ranks with their spades. The ceremony is staged like a religious service, the men chanting in unison. 'We stand here. We are ready'. A roll is called of the Districts represented. The chanting is resumed. 'Ein Volk. Ein Reich. Ein Führer. We plant trees. We build streets. We give the farmers new acres. For Germany.' To slow music, the flags are ceremonially lowered. The spades are held in line beneath the great skeleton of the German Eagle mounted over the Nuremberg Stadium. Hitler watches with grimly benevolent concentration. Then he addresses them. 'Earth and labour unite us all. The entire nation goes through your school. Germany is happy to see her sons marching.'

Night again. The torches flare behind silhouetted figures. Lutze (the successor to Roehm as head of the S.A.) addresses the Storm Troops. Fireworks and bonfires. Singing in the night.

Daylight. The parade of the Hitler Youth. Drum and fife music. Boys not on parade strain on tip-toe to see the Führer. Arrival of Hitler and Schirach, the Youth Leader. Goebbels is there, in uniform. Schirach speaks: 'This hour makes us proud and happy. We know no differences of class.' He turns to Hitler: 'Loyalty. We'll be loyal to you for ever and ever.' Hitler comes forward to address the youth, whose patterned ranks make wonderful shots to cut in with the Führer while he speaks. 'You are only part of the millions who are not here. You must educate yourself to obedience. [The boys' faces are seen in a sunlit soft focus.] Be peaceloving and brave. Don't be effeminate. Be hard and tough. Live austerely. We will die, but you are the future. The flag we have raised from nothing we shall hand on to you, flesh of our flesh. Follow us everywhere. Before us, around us, behind us is Germany.' Drum beats are synchronized with the applause, the drums seen in close-up. Hitler drives away through the ranks of cheering youth.

There are massed bands and singing.

A military display. (The Army being in its infancy, it is not very impressive.)

Massed flags in silhouette at night. Long procession in floodlight. A great spectacular assembly before Hitler, who stands on a floodlit dais in the Stadium. The German eagle is floodlit. Hitler speaks: 'All are here because their hearts are loyal. No one can understand us who has not suffered as we have suffered. The State does not order us, but we the State. The State has not created us but we the State. The movement exists like a rock. So long as any one of us can breathe, our movement will never be destroyed.' The pictorial effect of the massed ranks is like some spectacular shot in an epic film of classical Rome. There are close-ups of Hitler on his floodlit dais. He says: 'We will never give up what we have built with so much sacrifice.' The applause is accompanied by synchronized drum-rolls. The figure of Hitler orating is seen through the serried lines of men. Every hour, he says, we think of nothing but the German Reich. It is an impressive scene in the smoking light of the torches and the searchlights. Hitler gives the salute, bringing his fist right back to his chest.

The German eagle leads into a great perspective shot of the three minute figures (Hitler, Himmler, Lutze) marching up the wide space between the assembled ranks in the Stadium. It is daytime again, and the music is slow and solemn; it is a salute to the fallen. The three figures pay their tribute, turn and march back again.

Next, a procession with the eagled banners with the swastika, like tall Roman emblems. A mass movement of banners and flags. Lutze addresses the Führer before this assembly of the Storm Troops: 'We know nothing but the need to execute the orders of the Führer.' Hitler stands, a lone figure on the rostrum, silhouetted against the sky. He says: 'We have thrown away what turned out to be bad. Now the Storm Troops are as good as ever they have been. Whoever sins against the spirit of my Storm Troops will be punished. [All this a direct reference to the Roehm purge.] Only a madman would think that we will dissolve what we have built. We live only for Germany. You [the Storm Troops] are still the most loyal hands in Germany.' There follows the ceremony of the blood flag, the official flag stained with the blood of the Nazi martyrs. When new flags are presented to the Storm Troops, Hitler touches these new flags with the old in a kind of baptism. Guns are fired as he presents each new flag to the Storm Troopers. He stares at them, his face set and grim. There is solemn music, with Nazi banners on the screen.

There follows a march-past of the assembled rally. Hitler stands on a dais in the street. The leaders, including Goering, also march;

as they pass they leave the procession and stand beneath Hitler. The army passes along the streets and over the picturesque bridges of Nuremberg. Crowds line the route, and offer the camera innumerable portrait shots. Hitler stands saluting, seen from below.

The final assembly in the Congress Hall. The floodlights; the eagle banners. Hitler makes his biggest speech from a script, his face sweating, his arms gesticulating. He is evidently roused, excited, almost laughing to himself now and then with sheer pleasure in his power to stir so much applause and enthusiasm. His eyelids flicker with excitement as he pauses for the roar of appreciation. He cannot suppress the triumphant laughter his face reveals in close shot. He is much more volatile than in any previous speech when he had no script. He says that all the best racial Germans have joined the movement. Now he is here for ever. He is determined to keep the leadership and never let it go. 'More is required of you,' he says, 'than from others. I not only believe, I fight. Only the best shall become members of the Party.' (At moments there seems to be a touch of contempt in his expression.) 'We must purge whatever is bad,' he continues. 'The Reich is to last now for a thousand years.' (He gives a triumphant stare, and his lips stir with a proud laugh.) 'The youth is ours,' he shouts. (He breathes heavily, sweating in the floodlight, and clasps his arms to his chest.) 'The highest aim of nationalism is strength and toughness. We carry on our shoulders the State and the People.' 'Sieg Heil!' shouts the audience. Hitler ends by referring to the glorious tradition of the Army and the movement. He retires to his place amid thunderous applause; Hess comes forward, waiting for the applause to stop. Eventually he shouts, 'The Party is Hitler. Hitler is Germany.' The Horst Wessel anthem starts again. The swastikas fade up on the screen and blend in a dissolve into the marching men behind them.

The *Triumph of the Will* was, as we have seen, a production specially commissioned by Hitler himself. Between 1933 and 1945 the State, through Goebbels's Ministry, produced in fact some ninety-six titles. These films were known as *Staatsauftragsfilme*, that is, films produced by order of the Reich and financed by the state. By no means all of them could be considered as Nazi propaganda. They were, however, considered good enough for the reputation of the State to warrant special sponsorship, and they included not only the films already mentioned, other than *Triumph of the Will*, but virtually all those mentioned below.

The second category of films we should consider are those with

a National Socialist background to the story, either directly projected or implied in the line of thought behind the action. In 1933
Carl Froelich directed *Reifende Jugend*, with Heinrich George,
Herta Thiele and Albert Lieven in the cast. This concerned the
problems of a nationalistic headmaster, a strong supporter of Hitler;
he is represented as a lively, modern, virile teacher who has some-
how to convert his sluggish and 'reactionary' staff; in addition,
problems of discipline and leadership in the school are aired. Veit
Harlan carried nationalism and leadership into the industrial field
in *Der Herrscher* (1937), featuring Emil Jannings; this free adaptation from Gerhart Hauptmann's *Vor Sonnenuntergang* is set in the
Ruhr. Though primarily concerned with the family problem of an
industrial leader who wants to marry his secretary, many years
younger than himself, the film is infiltrated with remarks about
leadership in industry and the need for the workers to obey a
sound master. In the same year appeared *Togger*, directed by
Jürgen von Alten with Renate Müller and Paul Hartmann; this
deals with the frustration of the plans of an international concern,
which is trying to acquire controls in German industry, by a
patriotic editor, who is dismissed for his pains until the Nazis come
to power in 1933 and reinstate him with honour.

During the period of the war three films of some interest appeared
which belong to this category. In 1941, parallel with Hitler's secret
euthanasia campaign, Wolfgang Liebeneiner made *Ich klage an*,
with Paul Hartmann; this concerned the trial of a young doctor
who takes his wife's life because she is suffering from an incurable
disease. A friend who denounces him finally comes round to the
doctor's point of view on the grounds of humanity. The film ends
before the verdict is brought in, leaving the audience to debate the
justice of the case. This could be regarded as an unusually fair presentation of a controversial subject to appear during the régime,
especially as this was a state-sponsored film. Goebbels realized that
this was a difficult subject which required tactful handling.

More typical of films supporting the Nazi trend of thought was
Roger von Norman's *Himmelhunde* (1942), which stresses the need
for absolute discipline among keen-spirited youngsters taking part
in a youth gliding competition, and Alfred Weidenmann's *Junge
Adler* (1944), featuring Willy Fritsch, in which a rich manufacturer's

son is apprenticed in his father's aircraft factory, and undergoes the same strict discipline as the other apprentices; following a fire, he and his fellows work day and night to replace certain parts which have been destroyed.

A third category of films, and a prolific one, is that dealing with German history from a strongly nationalistic point of view. Some of the best productions of the period, many of them elaborate and spectacular, drew on German history in order to present it, truthfully or otherwise, as it was interpreted by the new approach to the understanding of the past. The films about Frederick the Great persisted—for example, in 1935 Hans Steinhoff's *Der alte und der junge König*, with Emil Jannings, in which Frederick Wilhelm, King of Prussia, allows a friend of his son, the future Frederick the Great, to be executed for a crime his son committed. This reforms the future ruler and makes him realize why his father allowed so terrible a miscarriage of justice to take place—because his son is needed for the future greatness of Prussia, provided he adopts a different way of life. This was followed in 1936 by Johannes Mayer's *Fridericus*, in which Otto Gebühr returns to his familiar role as the mature ruler. The film is primarily concerned with Frederick's campaigns; his defeat of the Austrians, his opposition to the French; his defeat of the Russians after they had encircled his armies. He returns victorious to Potsdam and, like Hitler, starts to construct the New Reich of his dreams. During the war a further film appeared with Otto Gebühr in the Frederick cycle: *Der grosse König* (1942); this presents the period of the Seven Years' War, and shows how the aged King takes matters out of the hands of his defaulting generals and snatches victory out of defeat. Second only to Frederick as a recurrent subject for films was Bismarck—Wolfgang Liebeneiner's *Bismarck* (1940) shows the statesman dissolving Parliament and imposing a press censorship in his efforts to unite Germany's forty states under a single all-powerful rule. He escapes assassination by an English Jew, Cohen; defeats Austria, and unites with her against France; and sees his plan for power come true when Wilhelm I of Prussia is proclaimed Emperor at Versailles. A second film, *Die Entlassung*, directed by Liebeneiner with Jannings and Krauss in 1942, presented the struggle between the seventy-five-year-old statesman and the incompetent Wilhelm II.

84

Other films intended to celebrate Germany and her historical and cultural heritage included *Das Unsterbliche Herz* (1939), Veit Harlan's strange film of Peter Henlein of Nuremberg who dies completing his invention of the pocket watch; *Friedrich Schiller* (1940), directed by Herbert Maisch with Horst Casper, Heinrich George, Lil Dagover and Eugen Kloepfer, which deals with Schiller's early struggles in the military Academy controlled by the Duke of Württemburg and his assertion of his rights to publish *The Robbers*; *Geheimakte W.B.1* (1942), directed by Herbert Selpin, about Wilhelm Bauer, the inventor of an early submarine in 1834, which is sabotaged by the British; *Der Unendliche Weg* (1943), directed by Hans Schweikart with Eugen Kloepfer, presenting the story of Friedrich List, the German economist and railway pioneer; and *Wien 1910* (1942), directed by E. W. Emo with Rudolf Forster and Heinrich George, which concerns the struggle between Karl Lueger, the Mayor of Vienna around 1910, and the Jew-backed Lechner, whose speculations endanger the city's economy.

The most striking of all the films in this class is Goebbels's greatest gamble with a spectacular, nationalist production, Veit Harlan's *Kolberg*, which was in a prolonged state of production from 1944 until the end of the war; it starred Heinrich George, Kristina Söderbaum (Veit Harlan's wife) and Paul Wegener. It became a refuge from war service for the German film-makers and technicians, and its production was spread over almost two years. It enjoyed the special support of Goebbels, who was determined in spite of every difficulty that Germany should be seen to be able to make a great spectacular film when the war was going against her. The historical parallel was obvious. The principal setting of the film is the city and fort of Kolberg on the Baltic coast during the Napoleonic war of 1806–7; the mayor, Joachim Nettelbeck, is determined to set up civilian resistance forces to defend his territory. The army is shown to be defeatist and corrupt, their morale virtually destroyed through fear of Napoleon. The film represents the mayor as a leading force in the revitalizing of the spirit of Germany to fight the invader and undermine his strength sufficiently for the peace of Tilsit to be signed. The last speech rousing the people to resistance was actually scripted by Goebbels.

The mayor's family is itself divided over the issue of resistance, but his heroic daughter, played without much character by Kristina Söderbaum, is his staunchest ally, and also helps to provide a romantic sub-plot. The interest of the film now lies in its spectacular battle scenes, which are confined to the last forty-five minutes. These are finely done, and beautifully photographed in Agfacolour. But much of the film consists of rhetorical, two-dimensional dialogue scenes and speech-making with somewhat obvious character per-formances by such well-known actors as Heinrich George and Paul Wegener. The film was completed so late in the war that regular audiences never saw it, its première actually never took place in the UFA-Palast, which was bombed out, but in the besieged fortress of Brest, where the film was dropped by parachute to give Goebbels an exciting propaganda announcement.

An extension of the historical, nationalist films were those which brought this spirit to bear on contemporary or near-contemporary subjects, including the period of the First World War. Gustav Ucicky's *Dawn* (*Morgenrot,* 1933) was made before Hitler came to power, and concerned the fate of the crew of a German submarine rammed by a British destroyer while saving British sailors from a ship they have sunk. Confined on the sea-bed, the film concentrates on the heroism of the men who determine to set a standard of courageous behaviour; two men shoot themselves to save the lives of the remaining eight, for whom there is sufficient life-saving apparatus left. The First World War is seen in many films—in Paul Wegener's *Ein Mann will nach Deutschland* (1934), in which two Germans in South America return to the Fatherland in 1914, enduring many hazards in the process; in Hans Zöberlein's *Um das Menschenrecht* (1934), which deals with the period immediately after the First World War, when the self-appointed bands of the Frei-Korps resisted the Left in Germany; in Karl Ritter's *Patrioten* (1937) about the fate of a fighter-pilot caught in France after his plane is shot down; and the same director's *Pour le Mérite* (1938), about a German squadron who refuse to surrender their planes after the war (a film which appears to be based on Goering's post-war exploit); in Wolfgang Liebeneiner's *Ziel in Den Wolken* (1938), the story of Walter von Suhr, a pioneer aviator; and in Gustav Ucicky's *Aufruhr in Damaskus,* with Joachim Gottschalk, a film of exceptional interest because it deals with Lawrence of Arabia. The

British are opposed by a young German officer confined in a fort under siege; the fort is relieved, and following the retreat from Damascus the remaining Germans go back to Germany.

Set somewhat before the First World War, Karl Ritter's *Verräter* (1936), which featured Lida Baarova (later to be concerned in a scandal with Goebbels),[4] showed how three enemy agents working in Germany are tracked down through the loyal action of a German soldier. Other films dealt with more contemporary problems—for instance, Robert A. Stemmle's *Mann für Mann* (1939), which emphasized the heroism of workers on a dangerous task constructing Germany's new roads and sinking pylons under water; Herbert Maisch's *D. III. 88* (1939), concerned with jealousy, followed by self-sacrifice in the Luftwaffe; and *Wunschkonzert* (1940), with the interesting subject of a young couple who meet in 1936 during the Olympic Games, are parted during his service in the Spanish Civil War, and finally reunited through a 'request concert' broadcast in wartime.

The worst of the German propaganda films of this time are those dedicated to anti-Semitism. These appear to have been concentrated into the year 1940, following the invasion of Poland and the final determination of Hitler to rid Germany of all Jews, deporting them to the East for slave-labour or, after 1941, for genocide. Two major feature films based on anti-Semitism appeared in 1940. The first was Veit Harlan's *Jud Süss*, a film which bears no relation to the story by Lion Feuchtwanger originally published in 1925.[5] The Nazi film, which featured Werner Krauss as Jew Süss, shows the expansion of the power of the Jew, Süss Oppenheimer, whose money supports the ventures of the Duke Karl Alexander of Württemberg, and for whom he acts as Financial Advisor and Collector of Taxes. He grows all-powerful, seducing the wife of an official. When the Duke dies, the people rise against Süss, who is tried and hanged after being suspended in public in a cage hauled aloft above the crowds. After his death, all Jews leave the country.[6] The other film with a similar anti-Semitic message was Erich Waschneck's *Die Rothschilds* (1940); this purported to show how the Rothschilds built up their financial empire in Britain through the £600,000 blood money received for German soldiers sold by the Landgraf of Hessen to the English army.

Far worse than these films was the anti-Semitic 'documentary' *The Eternal Jew* (*Der Ewige Jude*, 1940), directed by Franz Hippler. It is as vile as it is subtle, exposing the Polish Jews in the final stage of poverty and filth to which they were degraded by Nazi persecution, and presenting this as their normal, self-chosen condition. Following is a detailed account of this, undoubtedly the most vicious film the Nazis ever produced for public exhibition:[7]

The film is compiled mainly from newsreel material shot in the worst sectors of Warsaw and other towns in Poland into which the Jews had been herded by their conquerors, the squalid ghettos in which any street scene would reveal filthy and unshaven men trading such small goods as they could acquire and bartering them for scraps of food. In this way the Jews are 'exposed' as the vilest of human parasites, fit only for segregation from the rest of mankind. Their extermination is not mentioned, only the need to cleanse Europe from their parasitic hold.

At the beginning of the film the racial Germans are warned not to judge the Jews by those they may have known in Germany; these hid behind the mask of a civilized people. The purpose of the film is announced as exposing what the Jews are *really* like, the 'discovery' of them in their 'natural state', the ghettos of Poland. The cameramen have foraged round the streets for the worst-looking types of Jewish poor, starved and dressed in rags; the commentator remarks: 'Jews have no indigenous civilization; they are unclean; they are not poor, they merely prefer to live in a state of filth; their community life is on the streets; they hardly ever make anything for themselves; they do not want to work. Their only desire is to trade; their pride lies in haggling over a price. They have no ideals; their divine law teaches them to be selfish, to cheat any non-Jew. On the other hand [with contrasting shots from Germany shown] the "Aryan" wants to work, to make things.' Meanwhile, all we have been shown from the slums of the Jewish quarter are scenes of barter between seemingly sub-normal and unclean people, grinning foolishly at the camera through the stubble on their faces, trading a pair of boots, a pair of socks, or maltreating livestock hauled out of crates. At best they are selling vegetables from improvised stalls in the street.

In contrast to this we see, by means mostly of still photographs, the grand houses of the successful traders, who, the commentary points out, have raised themselves by such means. This, we are told, is why the Jews want to spread over Europe, so that they can succeed by merchandizing goods made by others. 'That is what they are,' says the commentator. 'Parasites—the eternal Jew.'

Then follows an 'historical' survey of the Dispersion, with accompanying maps. With the Wailing Wall as a symbol for Palestine, we see by means of animated maps the Jews spreading over the face of Europe, the Dispersion interpreted as the search of the parasites for grain. On the maps they appear like hordes of insects, while for pictorial symbols we see the rats feeding off sacks of grain and scurrying along walls. Finally, the maps show the Jews congregating in Eastern Europe, in Poland, driven out by the civilized peoples in the West who could not abide such 'pestiferous' people. Fictitious statistics are spoken in grim earnest: '98 per cent of the white slave traffic is Jewish', and so forth.

However, says the commentator, the Jews tend to change once they are in contact with civilized people. They attempt to assimilate with them by camouflaging themselves; on the screen individual Jews are shown, their faces become clean-shaven but cunning, their clothes smart. These, says the commentary, are second-generation Berlin Jews. They become socialites, rich men. There follows a long extract from the American film about the original Rothschild, featuring George Arliss. This early Rothschild is played as a rich merchant concealing his wealth from the tax gatherers. The expansion of the Rothschild family over Europe is then traced on an animated map, by way of introducing a sequence on the power of the great Jewish houses over international banking, over politics, and over the Germany of the 1920s—such historical figures as Rathenau, Rosa Luxembourg, both the right wing and left wing in politics. The Jews are shown (by mobile diagrams) to be spreading their grip over the professions; entirely fictitious statistics are given, such as, out of every hundred doctors in Germany, sixty were Jews. The commentator adds that while Germany suffered the rigours of unemployment, Jews became millionaires.

With the use of still photographs and newsreel clips, the Jewish grip on the arts is shown. In place of the great traditions of art (Michelangelo's Sistine Chapel paintings appear on the screen), the Jews created degenerate art (Picasso [sic], Gross, etc. appear on a montage). As publishers they specialized in pornography (pornographic covers appear on the screen). They imposed themselves on science (Einstein), the theatre (Reinhardt), cabaret (Curt Bois in female impersonation acts), film (Fritz Kortner; Peter Lorre in M; Lubitsch), and on singing (Tauber). The German people applauded them (Chaplin being fêted on a European visit) without knowing what they did. Idealized pictures of biblical figures (typical biblical illustrations) hid the fact that the Jews must have looked then much like the Jews of today. (A long extract from a Yiddish film of a traditional banquet celebrating the slaughter of the Persians.)

There follow scenes in Polish schools and synagogues showing the influence of the Rabbis who infiltrate, says the commentator, political poison in the guise of teaching Talmud law. Scenes from a service in a synagogue are cross-cut with (presumably faked) close-shots of hands exchanging goods under the cover of the wooden seating in the synagogue. Their message, the voice continues, is that of a so-called Chosen People; they preach the doctrine that a Jew must love only another Jew. Those who do not accept Jewish faith and teaching are branded by their fellows.

In the guise of humane slaughter to produce kosher meat, they kill animals brutally. A special caption introduces prolonged abattoir scenes, with a warning to look aside. Shots of newspaper headlines show how during Hitler's régime attempts have been made to stop these horrible forms of slaughter. They hide their disgusting practices (men grinning as the animals are slaughtered) under the excuse that their religion demands this of them.

This leads straight on to the display in caption form of the Nuremberg Race Laws, followed by Hitler declaiming before the Reichstag: 'If the Jews succeed once more in starting a world war, it will be the end of Jewry.'

The film ends with an idealized sequence showing off the beauty of 'Aryan' youth, with Nazi salutes, soldiers on the march, the Nazi flag. The commentator concludes: 'Keep our race pure. Racial purity for ever.'

There were, naturally, numerous films dealing with the Second World War. Typical is Karl Ritter's *Stukas* (1941); the story covers many aspects of the campaign in Western Europe, including Dunkirk, with the British shown in chaotic retreat and the French as utterly demoralized. A pilot who is shot down and survives in a dubious mental condition is suddenly restored when he hears Siegfried's Call at the Bayreuth music festival. The war was more notably covered from the German standpoint in a series of documentaries, for example, *Baptism of Fire* and *Victory in the West*. Shots from these films have been drawn on repeatedly for compiling documentaries of the war—the ruined rooftops of Warsaw seen from the air, the Polish civilian population herded on the pavements, dazed and watchful, while German soldiers stand around with their rifles at the ready. Another feature-length documentary of the kind produced regularly during the war was the Luftwaffe film, *Front im Himmel*, produced comparatively early and covering the air-raid defence of Germany, together with survey and bombing flights over Britain. Similarly, both the Army and the Navy had their propaganda documentaries.

Nazi Germany made its share of films with propaganda slanted against the enemy nations. Anti-Soviet propaganda began early in Gustav Ucicky's *Flüchtlinge*, set in Manchuria in 1928; it featured Hans Albers, and had Veit Harlan in the cast. A wartime anti-Soviet film was Karl Ritter's *G.P.U.* (1942), dealing with the adventures of Olga, a White Russian refugee from Bolshevism who joins the G.P.U. to find out who murdered her parents. Ucicky's *Heimkehr* (1941), with Paula Wessely, was anti-Polish; it showed Polish atrocities against the Germans in the town of Lodz, and the joy with which they hear the first German bombers pass overhead when the invasion begins. Veit Harlan's *Die Goldene Stadt* (1942) was anti-Czech; a young girl from the Sudeten area goes to Prague, the golden city, only to be seduced; the film ends tragically, and all the good people are German and the bad people Czech. Eduard von Borsody's *Sensationsprozess Sasilla* (1939), with Heinrich George, is anti-American, satirizing the American way of life, and in particular American court procedure and anti-German prejudice.

Some of the most striking films are anti-British, for example Herbert Selpin's *Carl Peters* (1941), and another film, *Titanic* (1943). The first, featuring Hans Albers, has a colonial theme set in Britain, Germany and Zanzibar in the 1880s. Carl Peters, in real life a mere adventurer, is presented as a fighter for the extension of German colonial possessions. Both the British and the Jews are shown attempting not only to oppose his acquisition of Zanzibar for Germany, but to have him murdered. *Titanic* shows how the only honest man among those responsible for the *Titanic*, a German ship's officer, determines to bring Ismay, the President of the White Star Line, to justice, since both of them are among the survivors. He fails, as one would expect. Ismay is shown to be determined to win the Blue Riband in spite of the grave risks to the safety of the ship. Max W. Kimmich's *Mein Leben für Irland* (1941), shows the British as oppressors in Ireland during the period of the Anglo-Irish conflict.

By far the most celebrated of the anti-British films is *Ohm Krüger*

(1941), directed by Hans Steinhoff, assisted by Herbert Maisch and Karl Anton. It featured Emil Jannings as Krüger and Goebbels himself participated in the script. German education in history had always favoured the Boers in their struggle with the British, and with his own kind of sardonic humour Goebbels in this film sets out to expose British perfidy and greed for gold in their dealings with the Boers, a machiavellian hypocrisy which extends from Queen Victoria to her politicians and army commanders. Churchill is seen as the commandant of a concentration camp for starving Boer women, while he gluts himself and his dog with food. The film, though slow, is exceptionally well-made, and Emil Jannings gives a fine, dignified performance as Krüger, defying the British in his old age and eventually losing his sight. The following outline of the film shows how Goebbels and his writers twisted history for their purpose:

The film is largely a flashback, Krüger's memory of the days of his struggle with the British. He is discovered in a darkened room in a Swiss hotel, and the press seek an interview with him, particularly the representative of the London *Times*. We see the dramatic face of the old man, like a great mask, with spectacles of black glass which shield his weak eyes when a press photographer flashes his bulb to take his picture in the surrounding darkness.

A nurse is reading to him from *The Times*. (She uses the *front* page for the news.) Among the things Krüger says as he listens to her are:
– If one repeats a lie often enough it is believed;
– With England one cannot come to an understanding;
– We retreated into the interior when the British came.

The film moves over to the main action, shots of the trek inland by the Boers slanted up to the horizon in sunlight and dust. Krüger's voice continues:
– We had only one aim, peace and liberty;
– That's how our youths grew to manhood;
– Transvaal, our Fatherland. Our blood; our sweat. Then came the English.

A sequence follows featuring Rhodes as a suave, plotting figure, handsome, with a black moustache and the face of a screen villain. The British are plotting to rob Krüger of the rich gold-fields in the Transvaal. Among the things said are Hitler's own words:
– One must be a dreamer to become a ruler.

Rhodes sends an associate to see Chamberlain in London; the Boers must be tricked out of their rich heritage.

An ironic sequence follows in which missionaries with pious

expressions sing the national anthem in the form of a hymn while distributing rifles to Negroes. The Union Jack is displayed over the altar.

Rhodes's emissary has been taken prisoner in the Boer territory. The smuggled weapons are displayed to Krüger:

– We Boers cannot afford such lovely weapons;
– If anyone smuggles arms into another country he must be an Englishman;
– One of the privileges of your nation is to be ignorant of geography when a territory is non-British.

Krüger confiscates the arms and sets the Englishman free. By now he has been established as an idealized character, his strength emphasized by means of heavily modelled photography with low-key lighting. An old man is introduced who has been forbidden to fight; he is to become a symbolic figure of indomitable age in the struggle with the British. In a tussle over the table with locked hands, he demonstrates his strength to Krüger. In contrast, an avaricious couple who want to sell out to the British become the symbol of appeasement. They claim that their Holy Ghost tells them they should sell. Krüger says that the Holy Ghost came from England, and throws them out. Krüger reveals after they have gone that when his father found gold fifty years ago he made his son swear he would never reveal it. Now, he says, the English will never rest until they have uprooted the Boers.

Krüger's son with his wife and the old man's grandchildren arrive from England. His son has been at Oxford. He is pro-British, but Krüger says, in reply to his son's protestations that it is quite legal for the British to buy up the Boer land:

– We must find people who can equal the British tricksters;
– England is our enemy (Krüger's voice echoes with prophecy).

Krüger then reveals that Chamberlain has invited him to London to discuss a treaty.

The setting moves to Britain. Queen Victoria is in her private apartments; she is a wily old lady. Chamberlain, complete with his eyeglass, visits her. Among the things said:

Chamberlain – Providence has called on England to educate small and backward nations.
The Queen   – We British have no friends in the world – they all think we're robbers.
Chamberlain – No nation is as pious as we are.

Meanwhile the Queen's Scottish attendant keeps her well provided with her medicine – whisky. Chamberlain reveals that gold has been found. A cunning look comes over the Queen's face: Well, she says, that is a different matter.

- If there's gold to be found, then of course it's our country;
- Only the British can become rich without losing their piety;
- Have our missionaries found sufficient rifles?
- Why should they not give us the gold, and let us take over their government?
- It must be easy to trick the old fool [Krüger].
- Treaties are cheaper than wars. Ask him to come.

There follows Krüger's impressive reception at Buckingham Palace, the old, bent figure as portrayed by Jannings, wearing full decorations, walks down lines of soldiers and ranks of courtiers until he reaches the venerable Queen on her throne. The cunning Prince of Wales stands beside her. The Queen says that she hopes there will be a treaty that will benefit all. Will Krüger sign? ponders the scheming Prince. Meanwhile the crowds press around outside the Palace. A man in the crowd says – 'Our Chamberlain will diddle him!'

There follows the formal ratification of the treaty between the Boers and the British – Chamberlain and Krüger signing. Chamberlain's final remark is

- The main thing in such a treaty as this is to abide by it.

The next sequence shows Rhodes complaining about the price that must be paid to the Boers. Rhodes decides to visit Krüger in person. He appeals hypocritically to Krüger to be the person to reconcile the Boers and the British. He tries to bribe him with a blank cheque. Krüger thunders – Do you think you can buy Paul Krüger? We have weapons! We are going to fight!

The Boers are marching to war, singing a fine German-style marching song and carrying anti-British banners. The crowd swings along in true Nazi fashion; men with drums; women arm-in-arm with the men; ranks of children.

Krüger's pro-British son intervenes with his father: it is better to hand over the goldmines. Krüger thunders back with his echoing voice: When do you join the army?

The mass battle scenes begin. They are in the direct tradition of Griffith, Eisenstein and the Soviet reconstructions of early twentieth-century war. The symbolic old man is to the forefront; so is the symbolic young man. The British charge; the Boers repel. Excited Boers converge on the camera from over the great plain. The running armies melt into a vast, kneeling throng before the father-figure of Krüger, his hands clasped in prayer, thanking God for victory.

London. The War Council. The sadistic Kitchener cries

- No more humanity. We must be without mercy. We must set up the concentration camps.

Meanwhile in Krüger's son's home, a drunken British sergeant attempts to assault young Krüger's wife. Young Krüger kills him, turns anti-British, and joins the Boer army.

The front line. The symbolic young Boer fighter is taken prisoner by the British.

The Boers evacuate Johannesburg. The refugees include the man and his wife who wanted to sell out. Krüger is told that British soldiers put captured women and children in front to screen themselves from the Boers. Capitulation was forced on the Boers by British cunning and duplicity. The horror of this news sends Krüger blind. His only comfort is to feel his son's face with his hand, and discover he is in uniform.

Young Krüger suggests that his father should go to Europe to visit the countries which are sympathetic to the Boer cause.

London. Queen Victoria is dying, but the Prince of Wales is examining the shapely limbs of the chorus girls in a Parisian music-hall. But he attends her death-bed, and watches her witch-like face as she lies there whispering.

South Africa. Kitchener orders Boer farms to be razed to the ground. Chaotic night scenes of the refugees in flight from fire and destruction.

The national anthem played diminuendo introduces the Dachau-like scenes of the British concentration camps for the Boer women and children. The food parade of the starving prisoners is contrasted with the Commandant of the camp, recognizable as Churchill, feeding rashers of meat to his dog. Churchill says that he must break the spirit of these women. A visiting welfare worker tries to make a Boer woman sign a statement that no atrocities are committed in the camp. A medical orderly swears to the prisoners that the scraps of bad canned meat are good. The Commandant kills the outraged woman—in self-defence.

Krüger in Europe, wearing dark glasses and looking very old. A quick montage shows him receiving lip-service, but no active support, from Holland, Germany and France.

Krüger's son approaches the concentration camp at night and communicates secretly with his wife. They are caught. The son next day is taken up to the dead tree on the top of the hill, which is etched against the skyline like Golgotha. There he is hanged, crying:

– I die for the Fatherland.

His wife is shot. The women, assembled for the execution, revolt. There is a massacre, and the black figures of the dead women are left scattered on the white hillside beneath the swinging body of the dead man. There is the crying of children, and the scene dissolves into a composition of graves.

This is the end of FLASHBACK. We return to Krüger as he was

at the beginning. To resounding music, Krüger declaims against England:

- That's how England subjected our people;
- We were a small people. Great and powerful nations will rise to beat Britain to pulp. Then the world will be clear for a better life.

The Nazi cinema as a whole contributed little to the development of the film. The great body of work which it represented—some 1,100 feature films and endless footage in newsreel, documentary and educational films (both contentious and non-contentious) [8]—contributed nothing new whatsoever, except, it might be said, in demonstrating how the film medium could be twisted with great skill to serve the ends of a wholly opportunist propaganda purpose. Goebbels's wisdom lay in his decision to keep his prestige propaganda at its maximum effectiveness by spacing it out and curtailing its quantity—except, that is, for the routine newsreels. His full-length documentaries were all the more effective for their comparative rarity.

The work of only one film-maker, Leni Riefenstahl, most ably backed and supported by her technical assistants, and sustained by the spectacular discipline and choreographic mastery with which her two massive subjects (the Nuremberg Congress of 1934 and the Olympics of 1936) were presented to her cameras, stands out for her creative contribution to the cinema during these twelve terrible years. Both *Triumph of the Will* and *Olympiad* broke new ground for the cinema. Not even Kon Ichikawa's great film, *Tokyo Olympiad* (1965), surpassed the work of Leni Riefenstahl. *Triumph of the Will* remains a kind of spectacular curiosity, a mine of source material for the study of Hitler and the organization of the Nazi rallies, a social and psychological phenomenon reflecting all the emotional naiveté with which the German people responded to Hitler's nationalistic dictatorship during its initial stages. But *Olympiad* remains a monumental study in athletics, an unequalled record in its own right well over thirty years since its first release. The opening twenty minutes are brilliant as propaganda, either conscious or unconscious; the international tradition of the Olympic Games is exploited to create a grand climax with the arrival of the flame in Hitler's Germany; there is no commentary, only a prolonged musical intro-

96–100 *Triumph of the Will* (*Triumph des Willens*), 1935. Leni Riefenstahl.

101–103 *Olympiad*, 1938. Leni
Riefenstahl.

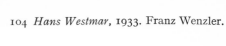

104 *Hans Westmar*, 1933. Franz Wenzler.

105 *Ein Mann will nach Deutschland*,
1934. Paul Wegener, with Willi Schur,
Karl Ludwig Diehl, Hermann Speelmans.

106 *Um das Menschenrecht*, 1934. Hans
Zöberlein, with Hans Schlenck.

107 *Hitlerjunge Quex*, 1933. Hans Steinhoff, with Heinrich George, Hermann Speelmans.

108 *Flüchtlinge*, 1933. Gustav Ucicky, with Hans Albers.

109 *S. A. Mann Brand*, 1933. Franz Seitz.

110 *Der Herrscher*, 1937. Veit Harlan, with Emil Jannings, Hannes Stelzer.

111 *Bismarck*, 1940. Wolfgang Liebeneiner, with Paul Hartmann.

112, 113 *Jud Süss*, 1940. Veit Harlan, with Werner Krauss, Ferdinand Marian.

114 *Grosse Freiheit 7*, 1944. Helmut Käutner, with Hans Albers.

115 *Träumerei*, 1944. Harald Braun, with Hilde Krahl, Mathias Wiemann.

116 *Romance in a Minor Key (Romanze im Moll)*, 1943. Helmut Käutner, with Marianne Hoppe and Ferdinand Marian.

117 *Der Grosse König*, 1942, with Otto Gebühr.

118 *Baptism of Fire* (*Feuertaufe*), 1939.

119 *Stukas*, 1941. Karl Ritter, with Carl Raddatz, O. E. Hasse.

120, 121 *Ohm Krüger*, 1941. Hans Steinhoff, with Emil Jannings.

duction composed by Herbert Windt to cover the impressionistic study of classical Greece which forms the opening sequence. We see the ruins of Greek temples and studies of statuary, nude athletes representing the tradition of the Games, and the passing of the Olympic flame from runner to runner and from country to country until the fire is lit in the stadium in Berlin, and Hitler proclaims the Games to be open. After this, the unique coverage of the Games begins, the whole film lasting some $3\frac{1}{2}$ hours.[9]

The complete film is divided as follows:

35mm Reel No.	35mm Footage	
PART I		
1	950	Opening sequence.
2	920	Opening sequence concluded (includes opening ceremony).
3A	900	Throwing the discus. Throwing the discus (women).
4A	950	Hurdles (women). Throwing the Hammer. 100 metres.
5A	750	High jump (women). 400 metres.
6A	950	Putting the Weight. 800 metres. Hop-skip and jump.
7A	670	Long jump. 1500 metres.
8A	880	High jump. Hurdles.
9A	950	Throwing the Javelin. 1000 metres.
10A	950	Pole vaulting.
11A	650	400 metres relay (women). 400 metres relay. 1600 metres relay.
12	800	The Marathon.
13	600	The Marathon concluded.
		END OF PART I
PART II		
1	900	Opening sequence and march past ceremony at the Stadium.
2A	900	Mass physical training and gymnastic exercises (men and women).
3	700	Yacht racing.
4	800	The Pentathlon (riding, pistol shooting and cross country run only shown).

35mm Reel No.	35mm Footage	
5	750	Finals Hockey. Polo. Association Football.
6	950	Three days riding.
7	1000	100 kilometres road race. Final of the double sculls, Coxswainless Fours, and Eights.
8A	900	The Decathlon (to the middle of the pole vaulting).
9A	900	End of Decathlon. Diving (women). 200 metres breast stroke.
10A	800	100 metres free style. 100 metres free style (women). Diving.
11	420	End sequence.

Chapter six

The aftermath cinema

For those who did not directly experience the aftermath of war in Germany in 1945, it is perhaps impossible to realize at all adequately the conditions in which the country found itself. The German people were for a while dazed and inert from the catastrophic nature of their defeat, following so closely upon the euphoria of Hitler's triumphant expansion of nationalism during the period of his un-hindered successes up to 1942. The incessant bombing in many of the great cities reached proportions which exceeded the single traumatic holocausts of Hiroshima and Nagasaki.

Those who arrived to occupy the four zones into which Germany was dismembered for control by the Allied military governments were, if they allowed themselves any normal human feeling, shocked and stirred as they moved among the ordinary men, women and children, the pallid wraiths of the bombed-out cities. Germany then was a country without a constitution, without a viable system of law, without trustworthy institutions, or means of government on either the national or local level. In May 1945 a task of the most formidable proportions lay ahead as some sixty million Germans confronted the four indifferent faces of their conquerers—the British, the American, the French and the Russian occupiers.

In the British Zone alone, barely one-tenth of the railway tracks were usable, while the rolling-stock was mostly damaged beyond repair. Many roads were impassable until major repairs had been undertaken. A quarter of the houses in the zone were totally destroyed, and a further quarter very severely damaged. Electric light bulbs were so scarce they were locked in safes during the daytime. Since these statistics included country areas which were comparatively unscathed by the bombing, the proportion of damaged property was much higher in cities such as Hamburg and Cologne, which appeared like deserted landscapes of rubble until one realized that beneath the piles of broken bricks and stone, people were living in the remains of basement structures. Where the shells of houses still stood upright in the streets—some with façades torn away and others with their upper storeys wrecked—homeless families clustered to find what shelter they could in those rooms which retained four walls and a ceiling.

Most fortunately, the summer months lay ahead. Conquerors and conquered began to establish the first, often uneasy relations in order to deal with the initial necessities of putting the country back to work. The railways and roads began to be made usable, rivers to be spanned by Bailey bridges, houses to receive elementary repairs, essential services to be restored, industries to be got working in however restricted a form. The Germans, as everyone knows, are among the readiest, hardest workers in the world. In varying ways, in the different zones, they were to be given their opportunity to rehabilitate themselves and their country. By the end of the year in the British Zone, 800 railway bridges were erected, and 7,000 of the original 8,000 miles of track repaired, while half a million damaged houses were made habitable. The economy remained in a state of barter. Food was in short supply during the first post-war winter, and the favours of women could be bought with a few cigarettes or a ration of black market food.

Meanwhile, the tragic farce of mass 'de-Nazification' was taking place, in which at least as much injustice as justice was done; far too many of the wily escaped their deserts, while those who had been more or less 'harmlessly' compliant with the fallen régime found themselves condemned. Of the major Nazi war criminals, after the spectacular Nuremberg trials of 1945 – 6, those who had been captured because they had not managed to escape from Germany to Egypt or Latin America or failed successfully to go to ground inside Germany itself, were put on trial in the various zones.[1]

Worst of all was the problem of the wandering refugees, the displaced victims of Himmler's racial purges and policy of racial resettlement. The vast two-way traffic of these unhappy people east to west, west to east, faced military government in the British Zone with two million displaced persons; by the end of 1945 one and a half million had been repatriated to their native countries, and half a million German agricultural workers received back from prisoner-of-war camps. But by the spring of 1946 the British Zone's population was three million higher than in 1939 owing to the refugees pouring in from the east, German and non-German alike, the mass of unwanted peoples. These, the foreigners who could not be absorbed into the normal population, became the pitiful inhabitants of the refugee camps, and a lasting problem in the years that lay ahead. In all, by 1955, some thirteen million Germans from the east were absorbed in the new, divided Germany—some nine million in the Federal Republic, some four million in East Germany, the German Democratic Republic. To these must be added the further four million who had moved from East to West Germany by 1961, the year of the construction of the Berlin Wall.

The German economy began to lift with the currency reforms of 1948 in the Western zones. After this, the great German revival began. But more than this, a cultural rebirth had to take place. As we have written elsewhere: 'A new cultural movement, a new press, a new educational outlook had to be born. It could not be, and certainly was not, achieved overnight.' [2] The new German constitution of 1949 brought the first phase of self-government to the conquered people.

Part of the immediate post-war cultural rehabilitation of Germany was to find expression in the film; on the other hand, cinemas are bricks and mortar, and had suffered as extensively from the bombing as any other property. In Munich, for example, in January 1946 barely ten cinemas were in use, as compared with the pre-war eighty, though the number was soon to be increased to fifteen. In Bavaria as a whole by the spring of 1946 about 100 of the pre-war 500 cinemas were exhibiting, while in the French Zones of Germany and Austria the number was about 370. In Hamburg, principal city in the British Zone, 20 of the pre-war 80 cinemas were in operation early in 1946.[3] The great and most significant exception to this was Berlin, that symbolic city, the divided capital. Here the authorities quickly began to vie with each other in their provision or promotion of entertainment in the cinema. In January 1946 no fewer than 170 cinemas were functioning in Berlin—56 in the Eastern sector, as compared with 48 in the American, 38 in the British, and 28 in the French sectors. During the anti-fraternizing period, cinemas open to Germans were banned to the occupying troops. During the next ten years, while the Eastern sector of Berlin saw little or no increase in the number of the cinemas, in the Western sectors of the former capital numbers rose to 246, virtually replacing at long last the pre-war cinemas in the comparable areas.

It is interesting to see what the policy of the occupying power was to the showing of films. German and other films in release before the occupation were immediately impounded and placed in vaults under strict security guard. The first films to be released for the German public were therefore imported prints from Allied sources. In the American Zone these films were considered to be carefully chosen for their 'escapist' value and for their gradual infiltration of new, more 'democratic' values. The result was an initial release of about fifty Hollywood films prepared by the Motion Picture Export Association of America with sub-titles in German, and including such films as Bing Crosby in *Going My Way*, Deanna Durbin in *A Hundred Men and a Girl*, René Clair's *I Married a Witch*, together with *Our Town, It Happened Tomorrow, It Started with Eve, Flesh and Fantasy*, and so forth. Anything which might appear to be propaganda, or to hint even at the recent war in Europe, was carefully avoided.

British films were selected for the British Zones of Germany and Austria by the Political Intelligence Department of the Foreign Office, and distributed by the Film Section of the two Control Commissions. The British did not worry so much about the inclusion of war films, and their sub-titled films included at first *San Demetrio: London, Blithe Spirit, Dead of Night, Rembrandt, The Lamp Still Burns, I'll be your Sweetheart*, and *The Foreman went to France*. Selected audiences were given special screenings of Laurence Olivier's *Henry V*, which proved a great success. As soon as possible, facilities were created in Germany itself for dubbing German dialogue onto British films instead of using sub-titles; this was done by German firms under licence in Hamburg and Berlin. The British, too, were quick to permit the release of old German films which were innocuous; the film section officers examined and vetted all the impounded German features and reported on their contents, with recommendations for the release of those entirely clear of any, even the faintest suspicion of, Nazi or nationalist intention.[4] There was naturally a great hunger and an even greater curiosity to experience foreign films after so long a period in which they had been forbidden.

In actual production of new films, fortune favoured East rather than West Germany. All production facilities were centralized in the State-sponsored DEFA (*Deutsche Film Aktiengesellschaft*, or German Film Company) organization, with the result that no initial problems of raising finance faced the film-makers in the way only too familiar in capitalist enterprise. Further still, the more important studios such as Babelsberg (near Potsdam) were situated in Russian-occupied territory, later to become the German Democratic Republic (D.D.R.). Also, raw stock supply problems proved to be greater in the West than in the East. Writing at the time in *Sight and Sound* (Spring 1947) the former German film correspondent, H. H. Wollenberg [5] said:

It was in May 1946, that, inaugurated by a function in the former UFA studios at Neubabelsberg, near Berlin, the newly-formed DEFA film company was presented with a production licence by the Russian authorities. A schedule of ten feature films was put into operation, apart from a programme of newsreels, interest and instructional shorts.

The next to follow suit were the British, who first licensed a German unit named 'Studio 45' in Berlin, and later in the year the 'C.C.C.' (Central Cinema Company). Outside Berlin, British production licences have been given to Helmut Käutner ('Camera Film'), one of the most promising directors, and Walter Koppel ('Real Film'), both in Hamburg.

In the meanwhile, the first films made under British and Soviet licences have already been completed and, therefore, afford an opportunity to assess general trends in the new German production.

By far the biggest film undertaking is DEFA. . . . Administrative offices are in the former UFA building in the centre of Berlin, which is situated in the Russian sector, and the firm has already expanded to such an extent that it now employs 1,300 people approximately. Its activities are favoured by the fact that two of the largest studios, which can still be used, namely, Neubabelsberg and Johannistal, are both just outside Berlin in the Russian zone; the same applies to the Agfa film stock plant at Wolfen. . . .

While DEFA is believed to have considerable financial backing from the Russian authorities, the British licensed producers have to stand on their own feet financially. British policy appears to encourage small individual production units as distinct from the big DEFA set-up.

It was a small group of courageous men, led by the film author Ernst Hasselbach, who formed the 'Studio 45' immediately after the collapse in 1945. When the British occupation authorities decided it was time to encourage German production in the British sector of Berlin, they turned to this unit and granted them a production licence which was handed over in July, 1946, at a small ceremony. Herr Hasselbach, during a conversation with Paul Ickes, gave a vivid description of the difficulties which had to be overcome in launching 'Studio 45'. Shooting has to be done mainly at night in view of the frequent electricity cuts. The artists and technicians are thus confronted with a very strenuous task, but all have responded extremely well and have no other desire but to work in films again. The principal consideration in choosing a story is the lack of material for sets and costumes, and the final selection of subjects is largely determined by these conditions. The technical studio equipment, however, is more or less adequate. The first production schedule included only two films, both of which have now been completed.

From these various groups came the first post-war German films of note—the period of the so-called 'rubble' films (*Trümmerfilme*), several of which suggested that much could be expected, a realist movement in German cinema which might perhaps parallel the neo-realist cinema in post-war Italy. DEFA was in the best position to give a lead, and among the earliest productions were Wolfgang Staudte's *The Murderers are Amongst Us* (*Die Mörder sind unter Uns*, 1946), Gerhard Lamprecht's *Somewhere in Berlin* (*Irgendwo in Berlin*, 1946), Milo Harbig's *Free Land* (*Freies Land*, 1946), Werner Klinger's *Round-Up* (*Razzia*, 1946–47), Kurt Maetzig's *Marriage in the Shadow* (*Ehe im Schatten*, 1947) and Erich Engel's *The Blum Affair* (*Affaire Blum*, 1946).

The Murderers are Amongst Us became Germany's first post-war international success. It emphasizes one of the most difficult problems facing the nation—the former war-criminal who, after the war, makes himself a model citizen in the hope that his record while in uniform will be forgotten. The former army captain, Brückner, responsible for wiping out an entire Polish village, is now in 1946 a good family man and fair-minded employer. His crime is revealed by a witness of it, a doctor who is now an alcoholic, Hans Mertens, who is saved from self-destruction by a girl, Susanna, a German victim of the Nazis newly liberated from a concentration camp. Brückner is pursued by Mertens in the ruins of Berlin, which form the macabre background to the film; but Susanna gradually brings sanity and self-respect to the doctor and impresses on him that Brückner should not remain the object of his private vengeance but be brought to open trial for what he did. The film was conceived and scripted by Staudte himself, and was remarkable not only for its subject, a significant one for the period, but also for its use of the ruins of Berlin, its sparse music score by Ernst Roters, and perhaps above all for the performance of a young actress new to the screen, Hildegard Knef, who played Susanna.[6] The film is full of imaginatively visualized moments, created out of a deep experience which the film-maker shares with his characters. At the opening a piano plays light jazz as the camera covers the ruins of Berlin, the crowded dance-halls, the over-laden trains, the derelict railway station. Gradually the girl is singled out of the crowd until she is in close-shoot; she is absorbing the pure pleasure of her freedom, her eyes full of tears. The doctor, finally seen in a haze of tobacco-smoke poring in a drunken trance over a chess-board, has also been first glimpsed in the crowded streets. Suddenly the words 'mass-grave' are followed by a spinning shot of the legs of ballet-dancers and then a scene of rain-drenched streets. The ruins themselves are the recurrent motif of the film; in some shots the rubble seems like a landscape from the moon.

The other DEFA films of this initial period were concerned with the more obvious social problems. *Free Land* dealt with land reform in the style of a documentary—the lands which once belonged to an aristocrat who has fled are divided up under settlers of peasant and worker class, who have to learn how to make the best use collectively of their restricted resources. *Somewhere in Berlin* dealt with the problems of youth and soldiers returning home after defeat and deprivation, *Round-Up* with the battle of the police against the black market in terms more nearly like a thriller. *Marriage in the Shadow* was another film which had a marked success outside Germany; in Germany it was premièred simultaneously in all four zones. It was based on the tragic story of the marriage of the actor Joachim Gottschalk and his Jewish wife, the actress Meta Wolff, who were driven by persecution under the Nazis to commit suicide together during the war. The fictional characters of the film face similar persecution and end their lives rather than face separation.[7]

The Blum Affair, directed by Erich Engel, a stage director, with a script by R. A. Stemmle, went to the 1920s for its subject, a notorious case of anti-Semitism in a German provincial town, in which a Jewish industrialist narrowly escapes from charges which are framed against him by the true murderer. The film, excellently acted but slow in pace, was intended to show how anti-Semitism, as well as corruption in the police and the juridical system, lay deep in Germany before the Nazis came to power.

All these films were, in effect, realist in approach. Films with a freer, more fantastic style were also being produced. *Wozzeck* (1950), based on Brückner's dramatic fragment about the victimized Prussian private soldier, was directed successfully by Georg C. Klaren in a near-surrealist style, with Kurt Meisel as Wozzeck. Nor did DEFA avoid comedy, though Hans Deppe's *No Place for Love* (*Kein Platz für Liebe*, 1950) was comedy with the contemporary background of the housing, indeed room or even cupboard-space, shortage. The lovers even try to get put in jail—only to be housed in separate cells.

Among the early feature films to be made in the British Zone, Studio 45 produced *Birds of Migration* (*Zugvögel*) and Helmut Weiss's *Tell the Truth* (*Sag die Wahrheit*, 1946), a well-made comedy featuring Gustav Fröhlich, about a man who wants to convince his fiancée that it is possible to speak nothing but the truth for twenty-four hours. The other newly-licensed company, C.C.C., sponsored an operetta, *King of Hearts* (*Herzkönig*, 1947), produced by Arthur Brauner. Of these films, *Birds of Migration* is the most interesting, since this also dealt with contemporary problems, the wandering German refugees seeking a place to settle. Another film of some importance was *Love '47* (*Liebe '47*, 1947), directed by Wolfgang Liebeneiner, in which a woman's life is traced from the period of Hitler's apparent glory until her final stage of disillusionment; she is only saved by falling in love with a war-crippled man who has himself had to face a similar disillusionment. The film had a brilliant performance from Liebeneiner's wife, Hilde Krahl, but was not free from a certain self-pity; the subject, according to Liebeneiner, had to be scripted in a week, since the film he had prepared to make was rejected by the authorities because it was not topical. Another British-licensed film of the early period was Rudolph Jugert's *Film without Title* (*Film ohne Titel*, 1947), with Helmut Käutner sharing a script credit. This film (though only partially successful through lack of real wit, invention or lightness of touch) had an interesting idea: a group of film-makers (including Willy Fritsch as himself) are discussing how best to make a comedy which will not affront German audiences in their present situation. A friend (an art dealer) and his wife (once a servant-girl) visit them momentarily, and the film springs partly from the story of their war-time marriage as it might have been had it been the plot of a film, and how it was in actuality. The interest in this relationship was that although the girl first met her future husband when he was a wealthy man and she a country girl who had become a maid in his house, after the bombing he is a destitute 'displaced person' while she, a farmer's daughter with a house and food, is a desirable girl to marry. The film featured Hildegard Neff (the anglicized spelling of her name) in one of her last parts, that of the young servant-girl, before she went for two years to the United States. Helmut Käutner had himself already directed *In Former Days* (*In jenen Tagen*, 1947), a successful film with a story of an old motor-car and the fate of its changing owners during the twelve years of the Nazi régime.[8] Jugert was later to direct *Hello, Fräulein*, which dealt with the tricky subject of American-German relations in the days of non-fraternizing.

Arthur Brauner, who was a young man of Jewish origin, was to become one of the most prolific of the film-makers in Western Germany. His first film, *Morituri* (1946), was set in a Nazi concentration camp. Later he produced, for example, *Die Ratten*, based on Gerhart Hauptman's play and directed by Robert Siodmak. A fast-growing company, newly set up under licence, was Real-Film in Hamburg, which produced *Nora's Ark* (*Noras Arche*, 1947), a comedy about a young couple who, lacking a home, go to live on a derelict boat. Another small company soon to grow, Filmaufbau-Göttingen, made *Night Watch* (*Nachtwache*, 1949), directed by Harald Braun and dealing with a priest's struggle of conscience.

The American authorities brought back Erich Pommer, the

pioneer German producer, from the United States and put him in charge of film production in their Zone; licences were issued only to various companies early in 1947 to produce films at the Geiselgasteig Studios in Munich and at the Tempelhof Studios in Berlin. The authorities laid down strict regulations governing German film production:

Films produced must support the reorientation programme, and their export to pay for imports of food and critical raw materials will be encouraged.... The film industry in Germany is to be reconstituted on a democratic basis, in an independent, decartelized form under the supervision and control of Military Government.... Policies governing the development of the German film industry within the fused U.S. and British zones will continue to be considered jointly by U.S. and British Military Government officials.... Particularly strict requirements have been established in connection with denazification of the film industry. Thus, Germans permitted to engage in the industry in important positions must possess high political and moral standards in addition to professional qualities.

Erich Pommer was quoted as saying:

We are giving technical help, but we are not responsible for the artistic contents of U.S.-licensed films. ... Production is going on with very young and inexperienced technicians. We aim at making B class directors into A class directors as time goes on. But on the whole I am sure that Germany will be a very interesting film country again. So far, these people are used to obeying; they must be taught to take risks. I believe in educating the public through the cinema. The Germans must make films which have some connection with the times and show a way into the future.

The first film to receive an American licence was *Palace Hotel*, produced in Munich, and featuring the inevitable Hildegard Neff.

One of the earliest films to emerge from the American Sector was also one of the best, *The Ballad of Berlin* (*Berliner Ballade*, 1948), directed by Robert Stemmle, with a script by Günter Neumann and music and lyrics by Neumann and Werner Eisbrenner. It starred Gert Fröbe as Otto Nobody,[9] central character in a cine-revue in the best Berlin cabaret style which debunked bureaucracy, post-war hardships, useless peace conferences and the like with acid good-humour. Otto, the innocent Mr Everyman, returns from prison camp to find a black-marketeer in possession of his flat. He dreams of cakes and ale and peaceful domesticity, but everything is denied him as he is torn, on the one hand between the political quarrels of East and West, and on the other by the dishonesties of post-war Germany. He ends up, after a fight, in a makeshift coffin, from which he rises to denounce his hypocritical mourners. The film was episodic and variable in its effectiveness, but was, and still remains, significant. Its satire was not without a certain sentimentality and even self-pity, but it was a brave film to make, exposing Germany's sores to the open air. Compared with this film, the rather heavy treatment of the subject of the Jewish victims of Warsaw and Auschwitz and their later troubles as displaced persons in *Long is the Road* (*Lang ist der Weg*, 1947), directed by H. B. Fredersdorf and M. Goldstein, was less effective than it should have been, in spite of the fact that its Jewish cast had in many cases suffered the very trials they were called on to re-create in the film. Egon Larsen, who saw the film with German audiences at the period of its release, wrote in *Sight and Sound*:

It starts in Warsaw's Jewish quarter in 1939, and shows its inhabitants going through the hell of air-raids, occupation, persecution, deportation and, finally, extermination in the gas chambers. A young man and a girl are among the few survivors, but the real heroine is the boy's mother who returns to the ruins of Warsaw to search for her son until her mind becomes clouded. She is finally discovered among the liberated prisoners at the Dachau concentration camp, and the film ends with an optimistic scene of the son ploughing a plot of land: one day he will be ploughing his own soil.

In contrast to some German politicians, who think the time is not yet ripe to confront the German people with such stories, it is a fact that all over Germany, with the possible exception of Bavaria, this and similar films on the treatment of the Jews under Hitler have made quite an impression on audiences. The feeling of remorse at what has been done by Germans, the feeling of shame and, sometimes, of guilt—emotions considered indispensable for Germany's spiritual recovery—are known to have been displayed in the cinemas more than on any other occasion.

Other films belonging, like *The Blum Affair*, to the tail-end of this period of post-war inspiration, were Josef von Baky's *The Challenge* (*Der Ruf*), *The Sons of Herr Caspary* (*Die Söhne des*

Herrn Caspary), and Helmut Käutner's *The Apple's 'Off'* (*Der Apfel ist Ab*, 1948).

The Challenge, featuring Fritz Kortner, who came to Germany from the United States to star in the film, had a disturbing subject —the disillusion of a German-Jewish professor who returns from exile in America to work in a post-war German university, although advised not to do so. *The Sons of Herr Caspary* was even more disturbing: Herr Caspary, an anti-Nazi, takes one of his sons into a comfortable exile in Switzerland, where he grows rich. The other son stays in Germany, living in honest poverty with his mother and becoming a squadron-leader in the Luftwaffe; they are, there-fore, loyal to the Nazi Fatherland, and are supposed to command the sympathy of the audience. After the war, the brother in exile is persuaded to return and work in Hamburg for an honest wage, side by side with the brother who had remained true to the Father-land, Hitler or no Hitler.

Helmut Käutner's film was a modern version of the story of Adam and Eve, with a cabaret-like treatment of the story of the Fall, which led to the film being boycotted by the Catholics. A modern youthful Adam cannot choose between two women, Lilith and Eve. Flashbacks show the ultimate boredom represented by the Garden of Eden, in which the protagonists go around clothed in cellophane. Everything desirable bears notices of prohibition—'For Exhibition Only'—turning Paradise into a kind of Hell. Finally the two women are fused into one to relieve Adam from the frustra-tion of his eternal dilemma.

The revival of short film-making had begun initially under the direct control of the occupying authorities. The Americans en-couraged Erich Pommer to make such propaganda films as *Hunger*, treated with much the same argumentative challenge to the audience as Paul Rotha's wartime British film, *World of Plenty*; the rural audiences were urged to speed up the production of food. In *It's Up to You* (*Es Liegt an Dir*), directed by Wolfgang Kiepenheuer, son of a distinguished German publisher, the audience was faced with a study of the German mentality from 1919 to 1948—how the way had been prepared for Hitler, and what the régime had stood for. Stuart Schulberg, brother of the celebrated American writer, Budd Schulberg, headed the U.S. Documentary Film Unit; he initiated a series, *Zeit im Film*, modelled on the pre-war American film magazine, *March of Time*, which had been the first to make sharp comment from the international screen on the rise of Fascism in Europe during the period of appeasement. The Russians, through DEFA, initiated a substantial programme of instructional and propaganda shorts, including a regular news magazine produced by Kurt Maetzig and his wife.

One of the first acts of the Control Commission was to distribute to the cinemas a special newsreel compilation, *The Mill of Death* (*Die Todesmühle*) about the genocide camps. As we wrote in our book *The Incomparable Crime*: 'Public reaction to the newsreel naturally varied. Many saw the film in silence without visible emotion. Some women wept; other laughed hysterically, then burst into tears. Men were seen sitting with bowed heads, covering their faces with their hands.' This, however, was a film imposed from without.

With the documentary film-maker Arthur Elton as adviser to the British Control Commission, young German documentary technicians were encouraged to put a long-dormant imagination to work on such subjects as the black market, venereal disease, transport, and local government. By 1948 work was well under way; Hamburg became a centre for the production of excellent documentaries, with a German Film Institute, founded by the Control Commission, already active in 1947 in the production and distribution of educational films.[10] One of the most imaginative acts of the Control Commission was to sponsor the work of the great naturalist and film-maker Heinz Sielmann, a world pioneer in this field, through the Institute.[11]

One remarkable feature film, only marginally a German product, was Roberto Rossellini's *Germany Year Zero* (*Germania Anno Zero*, 1947), produced through French sponsorship. Made with German players in German dialogue, which Max Colpet wrote into Rossellini's script, this grim film exposed the horrors of a half-starved population in which a boy, brought up where the only food is what can be scrounged or bought on the black market with money scraped together from ever-dwindling resources, kills his invalid father to remove a useless burden from his oppressed family. Remorse for what he has done finally drives him to suicide. As the film opens, a hungry crowd descends with knives on the body of a horse which has just died; afterwards, the action proceeds to its inevitable end —the mental disintegration of the boy, who is seen wandering in a trance near a broken fountain. There is no beauty in the rubble, no self-pity in the performances; only desolation and the abandonment of hope.

But such films were to have little hold on German audiences by the end of the decade which had seen the greatest military triumph followed by the most devastating betrayal and defeat the German people had ever endured. By now the escapism apparent in post-war populations everywhere turned German cinema-goers away from the contemplation of their problems. By 1949 what the Germans wanted was what the British wanted—*Madonna of the Seven Moons, The Wicked Lady, The Magic Bow*, and their German equivalents, soon to come. The popularity of the British Stewart Granger in period costume matched the popularity of the German Hans Albers, and the Rank Organisation by 1949 had two million marks frozen in its German accounts.

The tally of German home production was rising: 1946, four films completed; 1947, seven; 1948, twenty-six. By the middle of 1949 the Germans had either completed, or were in process of producing, seventy feature films. Wollenberg summarized an interesting report on the content of these films, representing the first three years of post-war production:

The total of German films released or completed but not yet shown or in production was *seventy* at the beginning of this year. Of this total, *thirteen* subjects have a distinctly political flavour, including two which present their story in a humorous or satirical manner. They deal with such provocative themes as war-guilt, racial persecution, pacifism, land-reform, and so on. Another *thirty-one* films (including fifteen of the light, humorous type) deal with a variety of contemporary problems, but without political implications; matrimonial problems, caused by the war for instance, post-war youth, readjustment of returning servicemen, black market, bureaucracy—and so on. The third category is entertainment pure and simple. It comprises romance, musicals, crime thrillers, escapist material of all kinds, and its total is *thirty-seven*, including fifteen comedies. Finally, there are *four* period and biographical pictures. . . .

The conclusion to be drawn is, that of the *seventy* films made, no less than *forty-four* (or more than half) are films with a present-day background and with a contemporary message of some kind.

But the period of social comment, self-examination, self-pity, and satire was all but over. The rubble was going, and no one wanted to be reminded of it. The growing German film industry was set fair for the box office. The talents which had shown their initial strength during the three years of social adjustment were soon to be stifled, unless they turned wholly in the direction of escape. The box office euphoria of the 1950s and early 1960s extinguished the inspiration of the German cinema almost as surely as Hitler had done in 1933.

Typical of the entrepreneurs who were to take over in the industry was Ilse Kubaschewski, who realized that there was a ready market in Germany for films of sheer escape. Her company, Gloria Films, began by acquiring the rights to old German films which had suitable entertainment value, and then developing from this into production. One of her first films was *The Trapp Family* (*Die Familie Trapp*) directed by Liebeneiner—the story being the same as that subsequently made by the Americans as *The Sound of Music*. This was to be the first of many *schnulze* ('*schmalzy*') films, musicals and other features such as those featuring initially the teen-aged Romy Schneider. Other trends were set by companies such as Lanzer-Films, which made harsh fun of soldiering under bullying sergeant-majors. How many in the audience looked back with serious nostalgia to these symbolic figures?

Chapter seven

The decline

With the currency reform of 1949, and the beginning of the West German economic 'miracle' of the 1950s, it was only to be expected that films dealing with the troubled past would no longer attract audiences when the day was occupied with hard work putting the country to rights and rebuilding industry. The original urge to conduct national self-examination was gone. The film industry was soon to become overstocked with box-office films—the huge back-log of unseen entertainment from the West. There was also great pressure to secure screen space for the growing number of new German-made films. In 1955–56, for example, the United States imported 211 films into the Federal Republic, while West Germany herself produced 124, with four more imported from the G.D.R. West German films were also gradually earning more through exports.[1] The whole tendency in the 1950s in the Federal Republic was towards over-production of easy entertainment. On the other hand, the tightening hand of authority in the German Democratic Republic ensured that political and social austerity was the principal characteristic of East German production. Few East German films reached West German screens during the later 1950s, and the period saw the virtual end of the interchange of talent which had happened relatively frequently during the late 1940s.

Conditions governing film production in West Germany which developed during the 1950s favoured the profit-motive only. After the currency reform, producers had to look directly to the wholly commercial distributors for financial backing; there was an acute shortage of any form of private capital. The industry, necessarily centralized under the Nazis, was in any case fragmented under Allied control, with some 150 small companies granted licences to produce films. There was no shortage of actual production; by 1954, West Germany, with 108 films, was able to take its place as the fifth largest film-producing country in the world. In a perceptive article written in the mid 1950s Enno Patalas analysed the typical films of the period as follows:

'Nur nicht denken—sich verschenken ' ('Never think—just surrender') sang Hildegard Knef some years ago in a film symptomatically titled *Illusion in Moll* (*Illusion in a Minor Key*). In doing so, she expressed neatly enough the attitude of the postwar German screen. The elevation of weakness, passivity, resignation, typifies the 'serious' German films of these years. To an objective spectator, the most obvious qualities in such pictures as *Meines Vaters Pferde* (*My Father's Horses*), *Regina Amstetten*, *Eine Liebesgeschichte* (*Love Story*) or *Geliebtes Leben* (*Beloved Life*), will be the lack of inner tensions, the weak characterisation, the absence of any inner dynamic force. He will be struck by their heavy sentimentalism, their conventionally lyrical interludes and tamely contrived plots.

The formula allows little room for positive action, for the display of reason or passion. These films are full of a vague and hazy emotionalism, the kind of emotion that is meant to 'come over you', undermining the will and the intellect. People tend to become little more than passive objects; it is fate, in the guise of social conventions or of pure chance, that ultimately dominates everything. Intelligence and initiative seem suspect in the German cinema, and only the rogue is allowed to display cleverness or common sense. The 'positive' hero has to be carried away by his 'beautiful' feelings, by the 'stirring of his blood', by his 'unerring instincts'. Faced with problems that demand evidence of will and character, he fails—but the failure is inevitably presented in the light of a beautiful 'sacrifice'.

This passive and quietist attitude is reflected also in the images and the dialogue. Stories unfold through fixed, static shots, stylised towards 'beauty' and composed in primitive picture-book style; actors move like the puppets they represent; settings and costumes, often elaborated with emphatic care, remain external, unrelated. Landscape and animal scenes are recorded with painstaking accuracy —a permanent characteristic of the German cinema—as are military displays, which fulfil a function almost equivalent to that of the musical numbers in American films. All this is symptomatic: pleasure in idyllic natural beauty, in the mechanical rhythms of a parade, is also a form of surrender.[2]

The films of the period were generally sentimentally fatalistic, many seeking release from tensions in the idealized pleasures of country life as distinct from the melodramatized evils of the city.

The growing prosperity of Germany led to a kind of paralysis of the imagination, succumbing to the old romantic wish-fulfilments in film after film which did little but debilitate their audiences. The great output of films from West Germany unfortunately represented a cipher in the development of world cinema, which elsewhere was seeing some of the best work of such directors as Bergman and Kazan, and the birth of new art in the varied work of Fellini, Antonioni, Wajda, Satyajit Ray, Ichikawa and Kurosawa, while the 'new wave' was about to break in France from 1958. Patalas, in the article already quoted, goes so far as to suggest that certain films of the 1950s in West Germany gave at least tacit support to the authoritarian dream—he instances *Sauerbruch*, the study of a real-life surgeon of genius whose patients are represented as having nothing to do but submit themselves to his inspired surgery, or Harald Braun's *The Last Summer* (*Der Letzte Sommer*), in which a young rebel succumbs to an all-virtuous ruler. Even the small group of anti-Nazi films of the mid 1950s were for the most part weak and lacking in full understanding of Nazism: *08/15*, directed by Paul May, which ends up by celebrating rather than criticizing militarism; Alfred Weidenmann's *Canaris* (1954), a study of the Head of German Military Intelligence who encouraged resistance to Hitler; Helmut Käutner's *The Devil's General* (*Des Teufels General*, 1955), and even G. W. Pabst's films *Ten Days to Die* (*Der Letzte Akt* [*The Last Act*], 1954) and *The Jackboot Mutiny* (German title, *Es geschah am 20 Juli* [*It happened on 20 July*], 1955). The most effective was, perhaps, Max Nosseck's *The Captain and his Hero* (*Der Hauptmann und sein Held*, 1955), which satirized militarism through the character of an intellectual. It was not successful with the public. There was another relatively significant film, Laslo Benedek's *Children, Mothers and a General* (*Kinder, Mütter und ein General*, 1955), which dealt with the last, agonized weeks of the war. It is instructive to contrast these films with one from East Germany on the same subject, Kurt Jung-Alsen's *Duped till Doomsday* (*Betrogen bis zum jüngsten Tag*, 1957). A more effective anti-militarist film was to come later in Falk Harnack's *Unquiet Night* (*Unruhige Nacht*, 1958), which dealt with the new Bundeswehr, the Bonn army establishment; the climax being the confrontation between a pastor asked to become an army padre, and the senior official who invites him, a man who during the war had ordered the execution of a deserter whom the padre had accompanied to his death. It was based on a short novel by Albrecht Goes.

Helmut Käutner's better work stands out almost alone in the overwhelming tide of bad films made during this period: *The Last Bridge* (*Die Letzte Brücke*, 1954), *The Devil's General* (1955) and *The Captain of Köpenick* (*Der Hauptmann von Köpenick*, 1956). *The Last Bridge*, an Austrian-Yugoslav co-production, dealt with a German woman doctor (played by Maria Schell) in the hands of Yugoslav partisans, whose patriotism gradually wins her understanding. She dies delivering them the medical supplies they need while under German fire, having made it clear to their leader that, having done so, she intends returning to her own people. Käutner directed the film with his usual technical efficiency, and Maria Schell managed to break through the comparative conventionalism of the script (on which Käutner had worked himself) and bring humanity to the part. The film, shot in Yugoslavia, was a very well-meant and, within its limitations, a genuine contribution to understanding of what the Nazi invasion of Yugoslavia signified to its people. *The Devil's General* (based on a play by Carl Zuckmayr) is concerned with Himmler's apparent attempt in 1941–42 to take control of the Luftwaffe from Goering;[3] the suspicions of the S.S. centre on an air-ace, General Harras, based on the real pilot, Ernst Udet, and played by Curd Jürgens, who is relatively open in his contempt for the Nazis. He suffers ten days' intensive interrogation by the Gestapo, but nevertheless attempts to help a Jewish couple to escape deportation, though they end by committing suicide. The General accepts the same fate when he realizes there is no escape from the S.S.; he crashes to his death in a bomber which he is piloting on test. The film has been criticized for lack of real understanding of the Nazi mentality; the principal S.S. General is a 'good' Nazi rather than a fully developed example of the true, dedicated S.S. officer, who stands in greater need of rational understanding and exposure.

The Captain of Köpenick (with a script by Carl Zuckmayr, based on his play, and with due acknowledgment to the pre-war film by Richard Oswald) was a reasonably effective revival of this old story, with a brilliant comic performance by the veteran actor, Heinz

Rühmann. Zuckmayr made the veteran officer's uniform, which the cobbler buys from a pawnshop, the central 'character' of the film.

One of the disappointments of this time was the comparatively poor quality of the last films made by G. W. Pabst. This was taken by the critics of his return to Nazi Germany as a necessary result of his betrayal, as they saw it, of his previous high principles. It is doubtful to what extent these seemingly 'left-wing' principles lay deep in Pabst's nature. The 'dark' films of the 1920s have their melodramatic streak; his best work was undoubtedly the two films which preceded his departure from Germany—the anti-war *Westfront 1918* and *Kameradschaft*, the latter the most brilliantly realized of all his films, though its message is not without a certain obviousness and sentimentality. Once out of Germany, or rather his native Austria, he established no roots and enjoyed no success; he failed entirely when he tried to work in the United States during 1933–36. He returned to France, where he made unambitious thrillers which were, however, successful. His dilemma in 1939 is described by Herbert G. Luft in *Films and Filming* (April 1967):

Pabst told me that he had his tickets for America in his pocket as early as the spring of 1939. His friends in Hollywood, who regarded him as an anti-Nazi, were waiting for him. But he never showed up. His long internment in France during World War I had become an obsession to him and he went to Switzerland when war became imminent; and two weeks before Poland was attacked he crossed into Nazified Austria. His associates, who at one time had called him 'The Red Pabst' (Pabst means 'Pope' in German), just couldn't believe the master would return to the Third Reich, especially since his second homeland, France, had recognised him as a leading figure in the cinema and awarded him a 'Legion of Honour'.

Pabst, it must be remembered, was a wealthy man married to a wealthy wife, who is known to have had no active antipathy to the Nazis and, it would seem, influenced him at this critical time.[4] His very mediocre film, *Comedians* (*Komoedianten*, 1941), with Hilde Krahl and Henny Porten, received an award at the Venice film festival of 1941. His next film, *Paracelsus* (1942), was made in Prague; it was one of his better films, and featured Werner Krauss. His last film during the Nazi régime had been *The Molander Affair*

(1944–45), with Paul Wegener; this was also shot in Prague and had to be abandoned unfinished when the Russians entered the city.

In 1947 when Pabst, living on his estate in Austria, started to make films once again, he was aged sixty-two. The film he chose to produce was *The Trial* (*Der Prozess*, 1949), which was to receive the award for direction at the Venice festival of that year. It was a study of anti-Semitism, pogroms, and an alleged case of 'ritual murder' in a Hungarian village in 1882. The central character was played by Ernst Deutsch, who returned from the United States to undertake it. The film, significantly rejected by the industry in Germany, was shown only in the film clubs of Hamburg and Berlin. After either directing or producing a series of indifferent films in Vienna (in one of which, *Ruf aus dem Aether—Call from the Ether—* Oskar Werner appeared), he attempted to promote in the United States a production of the Odyssey, with Greta Garbo as both Circe and Penelope; when this had to be shelved,[5] he went to Rome to try to promote a further production—a biographical film of Pope Bonifacius VIII, the contemporary of Dante, with Emil Jannings (now back at work, and turned Catholic) as the Pope. This, too, had to be abandoned; Jannings, who was seriously ill, died in 1950.

After many other ventures Pabst finally made in Vienna his film of Hitler's last days—*The Last Act* (1954), or, as it is known in English, *Ten Days to Die*. This film, which had seven script-writers including Pabst himself and Judge Musmanno, author of the novel which had originally excited Pabst's attention, tended to decline into historical melodrama with Hitler (played by Albin Skoda) as the key villain, and the rest as cipher-characters in his grip—except for the escape-figure, the young fictional officer played by Oskar Werner, who acts as the German-who-understands-the-truth, and who dies saying, *Sagt nie mehr 'Jawohl!' Damit hat alles angefangen.* ('Don't ever say "Yes Sir" again! That's how it all started.') Willy Krause played Goebbels, confined with his wife and children in the bunker, as a poignant figure, though historically his guilt was equal to that of Hitler himself.

Pabst followed this with his second study in Nazi history, the film unhappily titled in English *The Jackboot Mutiny*, which gives an entirely wrong impression of this misguided but heroic attempt on Hitler's life by a small group of high officers opposed to the régime. In this film Bernhard Wicki, now one of Germany's most successful directors, played Count von Stauffenberg, the staff officer who consented to place the bomb under the table at Hitler's conference in his East Prussian headquarters on 20 July 1944. This film, though like its predecessor offering to some extent a documentary-like surface, failed to realize the varied and complex motivation behind the tragic and abortive *coup d'état*. Hitler alone is seen as the root-cause of Germany's collapse; no one else is shown to be worthy of blame.[6] This was to be Pabst's last considerable film, though, already turned seventy, he remained in production for a further year. He died in 1967 at the age of eighty-two, his reputation still tarnished by his unfortunate decision to return to Austria on the eve of the war.

It was the actor-director Bernhard Wicki, the Stauffenberg of Pabst's film, who made what became in Germany the most celebrated film of the 1950s in which the 'unassimilated past'[7] was revived on the screen. As an actor he had also appeared in *The Last Bridge* and *Children, Mothers and a General*. In 1959 he made *The Bridge (Die Brücke)*, which went so far as to omit all opening credits in order to impress on its audiences that what they were seeing was their own history as well as that of the film-makers. Robert Vas, the BBC television director who escaped to this country from Hungary during the 1950s, visited Germany in 1961 and saw this much-discussed film with the German audiences of the period. He wrote in *Sight and Sound* (Autumn 1961):

. . . this honest, austerely planned work speaks again in the sober tones of documentary realism. It tells the story of seven youngsters in a small German town during the last weeks of the war. Episodes in their lives seem loosely linked, though rather too obviously designed to prepare them for a forthcoming trial of strength. Family conflicts give way to muted lyrical passages, 'bad Germans' to 'good Germans'; and there seems to be one of the latter in every family, in the school, even in the dreariest barrack room. But the school fails to convince us that behind its walls lies a whole time-tested system of Nazi education. So, when the boys receive their call-up papers, their outburst of joy comes as a surprise, a reaction for which their circumstances have not prepared us.

Throughout the film's first hour, the execution is cold and immaculate—too much so for the documentary truth the film is after.

The carefully timed conflicts are as surface-smooth as the baby faces of the *Burschen*, all wrapped up in crisp cellophane. When, a little later, these faces are covered with mud or distorted with horror, they no longer seem real.

For it is almost an hour before we learn what the boys are being prepared for. Hastily thrown in to defend a local bridge and left without a commander, they provoke an heroically uneven battle against the American tanks. Six of the seven are spectacularly killed. The film means to shock us by its harsh reality; but it over-reaches itself. The more horrifying the context, the more we realise the absence of that poetic grasp which would transcend the horror, until something dangerously close to apathy sets in. This is not just a question of *mise-en-scène* or simple talent. It is more disappoint-ment that the past fifteen years have not distilled from the subject a sense of the all-embracing, dramatically universal experience. Germany still owes us the *Westfront 1918* of World War Two.

The outstanding director of romantic comedy during the 1950s was Kurt Hoffmann, director of such films as *I Often Think of Piroschka* (*Ich Denke oft an Piroschka*, 1956) and *The Prodigies* (*Wir Wunderkinder*, 1959). The first, starring the Swiss actress Liselotte Pulver, had a Hungarian setting; the second introduces the Third Reich for background in contrasting the careers of two school-fellows, one an opportunist both as a Nazi and later as a black-marketeer and industrial tycoon. The second, who was never a Party member, gets by in life through his humanity and sense of humour. The author of both is Hugo Hartung. Hoffmann also directed *Felix Krull* (1957), adapted from the story by Thomas Mann, and starring Horst Buchholz, who had previously starred in a successful film dealing with juvenile delinquency, *The Con-Man* (*Die Halbstarken*, 1956), directed by Georg Tressler.

The most interesting example of the recession in the interchange of talent between the East and the West during the early 1950s was the case of Staudte. As we have seen, his first films were made in East Berlin for DEFA, though he was himself resident in West Berlin. After his initial film, *The Murderers are Amongst Us*, Staudte made others for DEFA, including *The Underdog* (*Der Untertan*, 1951), and a children's feature film, *Little Mook* (*Die Geschichte vom Kleinen Muck*, 1953).[8] *The Underdog* was a somewhat didactic film based on a novel by Heinrich Mann and set in Germany at the turn of the century. It is the story of the gradual transformation of a timid boy into a brutal authoritarian, a savage attack on the old concept of the Kaiserreich of Wilhelm II. The film has side references to current re-armament, and uses an expressionist technique; it becomes depressing in its earnest efforts to ram home its message. *Little Mook*, which was shot in Agfacolour, was a fantasy set in the Orient and concerns the adventures of an unwanted hunchback boy who achieves power and influence for good in a Sultan's corrupt court. By now, Staudte was becoming restive under the increasing controls in East Germany and, without actively breaking with DEFA, began to direct films in West Germany, notably *Roses for the Prosecutor* (*Rosen für den Staatsanwalt*, 1959), and *Fairground* (*Kirmes*, 1960), in which he dared to criticize the Bonn government in terms as strong as those he would have used, had he been able, of the government in the East. The body of a soldier, a deserter hounded to his death by an S.S. official, is discovered during the excavations in a small town preparatory to setting up a merry-go-round. The former S.S. official has now become mayor of the town.

In *Roses for the Prosecutor* chance makes two men face each other in an identical situation during and after the Nazi régime. Dr Schramm was formerly the prim, precise rule-of-thumb S.S. prosecutor made in the image of Himmler. In the last desperate days of the war he condemns a soldier called Rudi to death for stealing a little black-market chocolate. Rudi escapes in the chaos and after the war becomes a shiftless pedlar. Then once again he finds himself in trouble with the authorities, whose justice is still represented by Dr Schramm, now official public prosecutor for the new democracy.

Staudte does not play this situation for melodrama, or even drama; he plays it for irony. Rudi, who is only interested in keeping his pedlar's licence intact, has simply no idea of the political upheaval his petty persistence is causing for Schramm. In Martin Held, the actor who plays Schramm, Staudte has a superb exponent of what it is like to be a spider caught in his own web by a little fly who flounders far too much. This is a very civilized and funny film about an uncivilized and serious problem.

Other films of some significance promoted by DEFA included Kurt Maetzig's *Council of the Gods* (*Rat der Götter*, 1950), Paul

Verhoeven's *The Cold Heart* (*Das Kalte Herz*, 1950) and, much later, the film mentioned above, Kurt Jung-Alsen's *Duped till Doomsday* (*Betrogen bis zum Jüngsten Tag*, 1957). *Duped till Doomsday* is a violent indictment of the Nazis—the corrupt reaction of everyone concerned when three highly esteemed soldiers accidentally shoot their Captain's daughter and connive at letting the Captain believe it was the result of Russian bullets. The Captain orders the execution of three Russian girls as a reprisal, and the one soldier who breaks down and tells the truth is shot by his comrades. The film is made with undoubted precision and power, but ends by overstating its important case, and so weakening it. *Council of the Gods* is equally ruthless; set in the Rhineland of 1933, it concerns industrialists who are supporting Hitler (they term themselves the Council of the Gods) in order to win orders for armaments. The firm develops the mass-production of poison-gas. After the war, the same work is continued for the Americans; a great explosion finally reveals what is taking place, and a penitent research scientist, who has worked for the firm through both régimes, speaks his mind to the public. Like *Duped till Doomsday*, the film is very well made, but its undoubted power is again slackened by over-statement and over-rationalization of character. But the truth remains, that war is the active creation of men, not an act of historic fate. After these films, *The Cold Heart* may seem a mere fairy-story in Agfacolour; a young charcoal-burner in the Black Forest is granted magic powers and uses them evilly; he ends up a tyrant, cheating and betraying everyone in his power. Although he murders the girl he originally loved, she is brought back to life, and the heart of stone he had acquired at his own request is replaced by his innocent human heart.

DEFA meantime continued to produce its far more modest output of films—fifteen in 1954, twenty-one in 1957, twenty-five in 1958. In addition to the directors of the older generation, such as the late Slatan Dudow and Kurt Maetzig, the promising young film-makers included Konrad Wolf, Kurt Jung-Alsen, Janos Veiczi, Joachim Hasler, Joachim Kunert, Gerhard Klein and Martin Hellborg. Their films, however, were almost entirely ideologically slanted, as are the hard-hitting documentaries of Walter Heynowski and Gerhard Scheumann.

Chapter eight

The nineteen-sixties and the new German cinema

During the 1960s the German film industry, like the industries in many other countries, had to face the severe and quite unprecedented competition of television, though the impact of the new medium came somewhat later, even in the West. The results are familiar enough—the closure of cinemas following the decline in cinema-going, and the consequent introduction of sensationalism (especially in the exploitation of nudity and sex) as the industry's principal answer to falling attendances.[1] With audiences falling by a considerable percentage annually, German films sank ever further into a tawdry banality which invited a major revolt during the later 1960s by the younger generation of film-makers, who were bitterly resentful of the bad taste of the older generation of both producers and cinema-goers.

At the same time, a certain effort was made to encourage production, following the decline in the number of films made, which by 1963 had dropped to 63 feature films, in contrast with 106 in 1959 and 128 in 1955; of the 63 films, one-third were co-productions with foreign producers. The number of German films represented less than one-sixth of those available to exhibitors as a result of the rising importation of foreign films—particularly American, Italian and British. In the mid 1960s entertainments tax was a further burden on the cinemas, though films officially recognized as having some special merit carried with them a tax rebate. At the same time, the Government gave financial assistance to producers in the form of subsidies amounting in 1963, for example, to some DM 5·5m.—DM 4m. in 'premiums' given to producers with worthwhile projects, and the rest in the form of annual prizes. In some years the prizes were withheld for lack of films of sufficient merit to receive them, while producers often failed to come up with subjects attractive enough to justify absorbing the small sum available for premiums. DM 5·5m. would in any case only meet the *total* costs of between two and three average films; the Government had hoped to divide this subsidy (first available in 1963) over some twenty productions.

Though production in West Germany was to rise again, it did so largely through co-production with France, Italy and Spain; there were 38 co-productions, for example, in 1967, compared with 55 wholly German films, while in 1968 the total rose to 103, 50 of which were co-productions. But, indigenous or otherwise, the films made represented as a whole the poorest quality of any major country in Europe. A handful of established directors, such as Käutner, Rolf Thiele, Staudte and Hoffmann, endeavoured to maintain some quality in their work. But it is unlikely that many of their films of the 1960s will survive as more than vague memories in the 1970s.

In 1968 a new film law established a Film Institute, based in Berlin, to regulate the industry's affairs, including relations with the other Common Market countries and the problems involved in making any direct government subsidy to film production, an arrangement which the regulations of the Common Market would seem to preclude. Nevertheless, annual film awards in terms of money were being maintained, together with subsidy by premium to assist productions which promised to have merit. The German Film Fund Organization, established in 1967, awarded in 1968 DM 50,000 each to twenty-five films, with a further DM 100,000 each if the producer assigned the television rights of his selected films to the Organization. These subsidies were given on the understanding that the money be re-invested in future productions. But understanding of the word 'merit' is relatively loose—it is really synonymous with success, including certainly artistic success, if a film proves in any way outstanding—by winning an award in a foreign festival, for example. There have been many critics of the implications of this film law.

Among the more interesting films are those which have attempted to deal with Germany's so-called 'unassimilated past', the trauma of the Nazi régime. As this period recedes into history, a certain curiosity grows among younger Germans to know more about it, while the majority of the older generation who actually experienced it feel the need only to forget that they once had to live through it or played some active part in supporting it. On the other hand, film-makers in the Communist countries, including those of East Germany, are anxious to keep the memory of the Third Reich alive as a still valid contemporary political issue—DEFA production included films which reflect this, such as the work of Andrew and Annelie Thorndike. While West Germany, like other countries involved in the war, has made its quota of poor quality war melo-dramas, a few compilation films of importance about Hitler and the Nazi régime have been produced from the large quantity of archive material available. Not all of these, naturally, have been produced in Germany itself—the most notable of those from abroad are *Mein Kampf* (1960), made by Erwin Leiser,[2] a German stage producer who had been living in exile in Sweden since 1938; Alain Resnais's study of Auschwitz and genocide *Nuit et Brouillard* (1955); and the Russian film *Fascism as It Is* (1964) directed by Mikhail Romm, which contains a considerable amount of unique captured archive material held only by the Russians. Leiser made special use of a 'contrapuntal' technique—placing shots of Nazi militarism and atrocity against the bombastic speeches of Hitler and the other Nazi leaders. Resnais, alone among film-makers, has attempted the first film-poem, a requiem epitomizing with a passionate restraint the ultimate crime of mass-murder.

Walter Koppel, a producer in West Germany, Real Film Co., invited Paul Rotha, the British documentary film-maker, to go to Germany and compile from the archives a feature-length study of Hitler. The result was *The Life of Adolf Hitler* (1961). Rotha set out to examine those aspects of Hitler which were, and still are, the most essential to understand: what was the character of this man, the most spectacular and dangerous national leader of our time? What peculiar powers did he and his followers possess which brought about their ruinous period of power? In what other circumstances could this same subversion of human nature assert itself yet again? Occasionally the commentary becomes loaded and the clichés of natural hatred creep in. But in spite of this, the film is largely objective, and therefore both challenging and moving.

It proved difficult to separate the *private* nature of a man in Hitler's unique position from his public image as it was built up on the screen over the years by so skilled a propagandist as Goebbels. This explains why the sections of the newsreels showing Hitler's activities *before* he came to power seem more revealing, more memorable than the majority of those which come later and show him as the figurehead in the spectacular parades and demonstrations staged for pictorial propaganda. The study of Hitler himself is eventually all but lost behind the violent shots of war and the scenes of genocide in the camps and ghettos which the Nazis themselves recorded to their own perpetual discredit.

Another effective film on Nazi history drew on the film recordings of the International Military Tribunal at Nuremberg in 1945 – 46; this was *The Nazi Crimes and Punishment* (*Der Nürnberger Prozess*, 1958), made by Felix von Podmanitzky, Joe L. Heydecker and Johannes Leeb. Sequences were included of the infamously conducted trials of the German officers involved in the assassination attempt on Hitler in July 1944, and (cut-back in the English version) scenes of the actual hanging of two of the Nazi leaders condemned to death at Nuremberg.

The East German use of similar material appeared in Andrew and Annelie Thorndike's film *The German Story* (*Du und Mancher Kamerad*, 1954 – 56), which covered fifty years of German history and the struggle of the German Communists against the Kaiser's régime, the Junkers and industrialists, and finally the Nazi régime itself. The film ends with a bitter polemic against the re-establishment of German arms in the 1950s, an indictment of the policy of the West. Other films have been made as part of the polemic against the West, including films indicting men in high places in the West on account of their association, or alleged association, with the Third Reich. The Thorndikes were responsible for a special series, *The Archives Testify*,[3] which also promoted these indictments of men still prominent in the West.

Though interest centres today mainly on the best work of the younger generation among Germany's film-makers, occasional films from established directors have risen well above the low average of the rest. Examples are Frank Wysbar's *Battle Inferno* (*Hunde wollt Ihr ewig leben*, 1959), one of the best of the German war films in its reconstruction of the Stalingrad disaster, Rolf Thiele's *Labyrinth* (1959), and *The Girl Rosemarie* (*Das Mädchen Rosemarie*, 1958) both with Nadja Tiller—*The Girl Rosemarie* earned him the nickname of the 'erotic expert' in German films, with its updated *Threepenny Opera* story of a prostitute exploiting industrialists—and, adapted from Thomas Mann's story, Thiele's *Tonio Kröger* (1964), with Jean Claude Brialy and Nadja Tiller, and Hoffmann's *Rheinsberg* (1967), which gained the Lubitsch acting award for Cornelia Froboess. The distinguished stage director Rudolf Noelte made an interesting adaptation of Kafka's *The Castle*, though it lacked the obsessive claustrophobia of the novel. The exceptional emphasis on sex, often in the semi-spurious guise of sex-education (with filmed discussion by doctors or heavy-weight commentary by experts before the titillation scenes) reached its height of success in the celebrated Helga series, which began with *Helga* herself, directed by Erich F. Bender, and extended to *Helga and Michael* (Michael is her husband), *Helga and the Sexual Revolution* (*Helga und die Männer*), *Helga and the Sexuality of Nations*, *Helga and Group Sex*, and *The Helga Report*, directed by Dr Roland Cämmerer. Helga is a kind of specimen woman, with specimen marriage problems of her own in addition to those about which she conducts her research. According to Käte Strobel, Minister of Health, *Helga* has become one of the 'pace-makers of objective sex films'. Counterbalancing the large output of erotic films with such titles as *Undress Yourself*, *Doll* and *The Girl with the Sexth Sense*,[4] are the semi-documentaries with enacted love-scenes, such as *The Wonder of Love*, directed by F. J. Gottlieb and promoted by the successful sex-education columnist, Oswalt Kolle.

A new generation of directors is beginning to establish itself, and it is here that the long-awaited regeneration of the art of the film in Germany may lie. The directors who already count in this movement of individualists include Alexander Kluge (born 1932), Edgar Reitz (born 1932; Kluge's director of photography for *Yesterday Girl*), Peter and Ulrich Schamoni (born 1934 and 1939), Volker Schlöndorff (born 1939; former assistant in France to both Louis Malle and Resnais), Jean-Marie Straub (born 1933) and Roger Fritz. Alongside these already fully established film-makers are others whose work has been well noticed, such as Hans-Jürgen Pohland, Will Tremper, Franz-Josef Spieker, and May Spils who, with Peter Schamoni as producer and Werner Enke as the comedy star, directed

122–124 *The Murderers are Amongst Us*
(*Die Mörder sind unter Uns*), 1946.
Wolfgang Staudte, with Hildegard Knef
and Robert Forsch.

125 *Free Land* (*Freies Land*), 1946.
Milo Harbig.

△

126 *Somewhere in Berlin* (*Irgendwo in Berlin*), 1946. Gerhard Lamprecht.

127, 128 *Marriage in the Shadow* (*Ehe im Schatten*), 1947. Kurt Maetzig, with Ilse Steppat.

129 *In Former Days* (*In Jenen Tagen*), 1947. Helmut Käutner.

130 *The Blum Affair (Affaire Blum)*, 1946. Erich Engel.

131 *Wozzeck*, 1950. Georg C. Klaren, with Kurt Meisel.

132 *Tell the Truth (Sag die Wahrheit)*, 1946. Helmut Weiss, with Gustav Fröhlich.

133 *Birds of Migration*
(*Zugvögel*), 1946.
Studio 45.

134, 135 *The Ballad of
Berlin* (*Berliner
Ballade*), 1948. Robert
Stemmle, with Gert
Fröbe.

136 *Germany Year Zero*
(*Germania Anno Zero*), 1947.
Roberto Rossellini.

137–8 *Report on the*
Refugee Situation, 1947.
(British Control
Commission.)

139 *The Trial (Der Prozess)*, 1949. G. W. Pabst, with Ernst Deutsch.

140, 141 *Ten Days to Die (Der Letzte Akt)*, 1954. G. W. Pabst.

142 *The Devil's General* (*Des Teufels General*), 1955. Helmut Käutner, with Curd Jürgens, Victor de Kowa.

143 *Children, Mothers and a General* (*Kinder, Mütter und ein General*), 1955. Laslo Benedek, with Teresa Giehse, Bernhard Wicki.

144 *Roses for the Prosecutor* (*Rosen für den Staatsanwalt*), 1959. Wolfgang Staudte.

145 *The Bridge* (*Die Brücke*), 1959. Bernhard Wicki, with Werner Peters.

146 *The Underdog (Der Untertan)*, 1951. Wolfgang Staudte, with Werner Peters.

147 *Council of the Gods (Rat der Götter)*, 1950. Kurt Maetzig.

148 *Professor Mamlock*, 1961. Konrad Wolf.

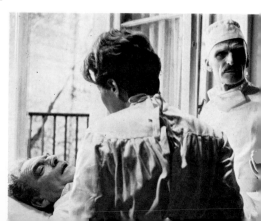

149 *The Wonder of Love*, 1967. Oswalt Kolle with Katarina Haertel and Regis Vallee.

150 *The Castle* (*Das Schloss*), 1968. Rudolf Noelte, with Maximilian Schell, Friedrich Maurer.

151 *Cardillac*, 1969. Edgar Reitz.

152 *Labyrinth*, 1959. Rolf Thiele, with Georgia Gale.

153 *Young Törless (Der Junge Törless)*, 1966. Volker Schlöndorff, Pitoeff and Delphine Seyrig.

154 *I often think of Piroschka (Ich denke oft an Piroschka)*, 1956. Kurt Hoffmann, with Liselotte Pulver.

155 *The Inn in the Spessart (Das Wirtshaus im Spessart)*, 1957. Kurt Hoffmann, with Curt Bois, Hubert von Meyerinck.

156, 157 *Yesterday Girl* (*Abschied von Gestern*), 1966. Alexander Kluge, with Alexandra Kluge, Günter Mack.

158, 159 *Artistes at the Top of the Big Top: Disorientated* (*Die Artisten in der Zirkuskuppel: Ratlos*), 1968. Alexander Kluge, with Hannelore Hoger.

160 *Come to the point, Darling* (*Zur Sache, Schätzchen*), 1969. May Spils, with Werner Enke, Uschi Glas.

161 *The Virgin from Bamberg* (*Die Jungfrau von Bamberg*), 1969. Marran Gosov, with Gila von Weitershausen and Dieter Augustin.

162, 163 *Marriage Trouble* (*Alle Jahre Wieder*), 1967. Ulrich Schamoni, with Sabine Sinjen and Hans-Dieter Schwarze.

Zur Sache, Schätzchen (*Come to the point, Darling*), a great box-office success. The brilliant cartoonist from Yugoslavia, Vlado Kristl, went to work in Germany, and appears to remain dedicated to this avant-garde work. Behind these serious directors and their colleagues seethes an even younger generation of amateur and semi-amateur 'underground' film-makers whose films reflect the same obsessive 'protests' as the work of underground film-makers everywhere, often accompanying their political and pseudo-pornographic demonstrations on the screen with similar activities in the auditorium, as at the 1969 Oberhausen festival.

Schlöndorff, the Schamonis, and Reitz make films which break new ground but belong to the mainstream of the new, more enlightened commercial cinema. Schlöndorff's initial films proved him an important film-maker for Germany: *Young Törless* (*Der Junge Törless*, 1966) is the story of a sensitive boy's psychological reaction to his period at a para-military academy in the Austro-Hungarian empire, adapted from the novel by Robert Musil; *A Degree of Murder* (*Mord und Totschlag*, 1966) is a cool, objective study of the way in which a waitress rids herself of the body of a former lover whom she shoots; *Michael Kohlhaas* (*Michal Kohlhaas—Der Rebell*, 1969) with David Warner and Anna Karina, is set in sixteenth-century Germany and based on a story by Heinrich von Kleist which is concerned with an individual's abortive fight for justice and his rights, a period story to which Schlöndorff tries to give an unfortunate contemporary slant. Schlöndorff's work reveals him to be a film-maker of great technical brilliance with meticulous style which is more successful in the first two of these films than in the third.

Roger Fritz, a photographer and actor as well as a producer and director of film, worked as a first assistant to Visconti on *The Leopard*. After making short films he co-directed *Girls, Girls* (*Mädchen, Mädchen*, 1966), which concerns the moral and sexual dilemma of a young girl after leaving a reformatory. Fritz then acted in Marran Gosov's psychological study of a marriage, *Zuckerbrot und Peitsche*, and after this directed another film, *Run, Rabbit Run* (*Häschen in der Grube*, 1969), about a girl who steals her mother's lover. Both Fritz's films feature Helga Anders; though they deal with the younger generation, these films do not claim to reflect any remarkable personal style or technique of presentation. Edgar Reitz, another photographer, asserts his individuality more strongly; his film, *Lust for Love*, he links with the 'myth' of the 'feminine mystique' put forward in the American sociologist Betty Friedan's celebrated book; the central character of the film reflects or reacts to the mystique in the course of her two marriages. His film *Cardillac* (1969) is derived from a tale by Hoffmann about a master jeweller who murders his clients in order to retrieve the masterpieces of his craftsmanship which he has sold to them. These he exhibits for his delight on the bare torso of his dark-skinned daughter, child of a liaison with a black mistress from Guadeloupe. The film has a certain rhetorical beauty, an exaggeration which suits the character of this man, who finally kills himself in an electric chair of his own construction. It is beautifully photographed, especially when the nude girl is modelling the jewellery.

The Schamoni brothers were, with Alexander Kluge and others, leading members of a movement of younger film-makers which in the early 1960s founded the Oberhausen Group. They were determined to create a new era or 'wave' in German cinema—Bubis Kino, as they called it. Ulrich Schamoni's first feature film, *It* (*Es*, 1966), used the wildly free camera style of *cinévérité* in this study of the prejudices surrounding abortion. His elder brother Peter Schamoni's *Schonzeit für Füchse* (1966) dealt with the generation gap.

Alexander Kluge acted as the diplomat of the group; a doctor of law, he had the ear of officials in Bonn, and he was instrumental both in setting up a film school at Ulm and in establishing the Kuratorium Junger Deutscher Film, an official fund of some DM 2m. to make loans to the more promising younger film-makers. Beneficiaries from the fund have included Spieker, Kristl and Kluge himself, whose first feature film, *Yesterday Girl* (*Abschied von Gestern*, 1966), received a grant of DM 300,000 towards its costs. Kluge, who is also an established writer, adapted this film from his book *Lebensläufe* which is about a girl who leaves East Germany for the West, though her search for a new way of life in the comparative freedom of the Federal Republic does not match her expectations. Kluge is equally critical of both East and West. As a film-maker he creates imaginative, imagistic feature-documentaries, in which contemporary society is explored through the dilemma of an individual. He is considered to be influenced by Godard, but his style and viewpoint differ radically. The girl from East Germany, who is highly intelligent, takes to regular stealing and the like as a direct result of the unimaginative treatment she receives after her arrest for a petty theft. She adopts a vagrant, aimless life, becoming the casual mistress of a series of men, though loved by none. The film sounds grey and drab, but it is made with such charm and intelligence that its humanity is what impresses one most of all. Anita is a 'yesterday girl' because she is Jewish, and Kluge is out to show that no society can change as radically as it may think. A modern welfare society can be frustrating and oppressive, though what is done is disguised as humane. In the end Anita finds that she prefers to judge herself rather than be judged by others, and gives herself up in order to do so. Anita was played with great sensitivity by Kluge's sister, Alexandra.

German society was equally the subject of analytical observation in Kluge's second feature film, with its allusive title, *Artistes at the Top of the Big Top: Disorientated* (*Die Artisten in der Zirkuskuppel: Ratlos*, 1968). Leni Peickert attempts to create a Utopian society within the enclosed world she knows best, the circus. She soon finds she is attempting the impossible; the circus, like the larger world it symbolizes, is incapable of such drastic rehabilitation; the past invariably inhibits the present, and compromise is forced upon the idealist. The elephants, who cannot forget, insist on performing the same routines. The film is an essay in the exposition of an idea through visual imagery; it demonstrates a philosophy of society. Social changes may be achieved only by a process of gradation. Kluge's resemblance to Godard, whose films adopt a dialectical technique, lies only in the fact that he uses the medium for an elliptical, allusive demonstration of ideas.

Individualists in the new German cinema include Will Tremper, a distinguished journalist and screenwriter, and Jean-Marie Straub. Tremper in *Playgirl* (1966) created a film on the basis largely of improvisation; the theme is similar to *Darling*, and the protagonist was played by a comparatively unknown actress, Eva Renzi, with great sympathy and understanding of the girl's character. Having completed the film, Tremper was forced to distribute it himself, and made a box-office success out of his venture.

Straub, a Frenchman living in Munich, is isolated from any recognizable movement in the cinema, commercial or otherwise. He has the austerity and remoteness of a Bresson or a Dreyer. His films are cool (in the sense in which McLuhan uses the word), demanding the maximum from their audiences, giving out little or nothing unless the viewer himself works for it. The short films adapted from the ironic stories of Heinrich Böll, *Machorka Muffl* (1962) and *Unreconciled* (*Nicht Versöhnt*, 1965), expose the more extreme right-wing elements in West German political, social and industrial life by letting them utter their absurdities in tones so withdrawn and understated as to be completely drained of any trace of conventional dramatic feeling, although what they say has a certain quality of immediacy because it is directly recorded, not post-synchronized. The leading characters bear names which caricature their natures: Colonel Machorka Muffl, for example, might be rendered Colonel Stuffy. Of *The Chronicle of Anna Magdalena Bach* (*Die Chronik der Anna Magdalena Bach*, 1967), Straub has been quoted as saying: 'My film about Bach is Marxist. It is not a documentary, though some people think that it is. You should look at it like people viewing Lumière's first work. Watch the movement of the hands, of the wigs. And if you don't like what you see, please leave quietly because others may want to stay, to concentrate.' Using the same cool method of presentation, the film shows a great musician's difficulties in his relationship to the society of his time, as related in the diary left by his wife.

Munich has become the centre for much new film-making in Germany; the producer Rob Houwer has done a great deal to help the younger film-makers to produce their initial work, while Haro Senft was among those who helped found the movement. Not only are Kluge, Reitz, Fritz, Straub, Kristl, and Peter Schamoni based in Munich, but many other new directors work from there, such as Werner Herzog (*Signs of Life*, 1968, and *Even Dwarfs Start Small*, 1970), Franz-Josef Spieker (*Wilder Reiter GmbH*, 1966), Peter Fleischmann (*Jagdszenen in Niederbayern*, 1968), Johannes Schauf (*Tatowierung*, 1967), Hans Rudolf Strobel and Heinz Tichawsky (*A Marriage*, 1967–68), Eckhard Schmidt (*Mädchen, Mädchen*, 1966— with Roger Fritz—and *Nach Amerika*, 1967) and experimentalists like Ferdinand Khittl (*Die Parallelstrasse*, 1961) and Helmuth

Costard, the protagonist of the underground, with his 'banned' short, *Besonders Wertvoll* (1967). Klaus Lemke (*48 Hours in Acapulco*, 1970, with Dieter Geissler) and Rolf Thomé are more influenced in their productions by the American action film. In Berlin there is Will Tremper and producer-director Hans-Jürgen Pohland, who produced, among other films, *Brot der frühen Jahre* (1962), directed by Herbert Vesely and based on the novel by Heinrich Böll, and *Katz und Maus*, 1966. The collective work of all these directors reveals that a quarter of a century after the fall of Hitler the German film may well return to its former high place in world cinema.

Notes

CHAPTER ONE pages I – IO

[1] Oskar Messter (1866–1943). Designed a projector known as the Kine-matograph, marketed as early as 1896. Published his biography *Mein Weg mit dem Film* in 1936.

[2] Max Skladanowsky (1863–1939). His projector was a dual apparatus, each synchronized, alternating projector operating at eight frames a second. The apparatus and archives of the Skladanowskys are preserved now at the G.D.R. Film Institute in East Berlin.

[3] H. H. Wollenberg in *Fifty Years of German Film* refers to an academic investigation made as early as 1913 which revealed no less than three hundred new cinemas opened in Berlin in 1908, and states that this was symptomatic of the country as a whole.

[4] Carl Froelich (1875–1953). Froelich was later to occupy a key position in the film industry under Hitler. He began as an electrician for Messter, and was a cameraman before he became a director in 1902, filming a five-minute dance of Salomé direct from the stage.

[5] Max Mack (b. 1884). A distinguished director during the silent period, Mack, a Jew, was forced to leave Germany in 1933, and settled in Britain. In 1913 he filmed Sudermann's play *Katzensteg*, which gave Paul Leni his first assignment as an art director.

[6] Albert Bassermann (1867–1948). He became a refugee from Hitler's Germany; he appeared in a number of Hollywood films, including *Foreign Correspondent*, and, in Britain, in *The Red Shoes*.

[7] Paul Wegener (1874–1948). An actor rather than a film-maker, Wegener was one of the stars in Reinhardt's theatre.

[8] Henny Porten (1890–1960). After a brilliant career as Germany's most popular actress of the silent screen, Henny Porten (in spite of her ideal Germanic blonde appearance) suffered badly under Hitler for her loyalty to her husband, Dr von Kaufmann, who had Jewish blood. After the war she

failed to achieve a comeback in West Germany, but starred in *Carola Lamberti* in East Germany, 1955.

[9] Asta Nielsen (b. 1883). Her most popular film in Germany was *Engelein* (1911), a comedy in which she played a pre-war 'flapper'.

[10] Paul Davidson (1867–1927). Starting in the clothing business, he entered the industry as a cinema proprietor in 1905. He owned several important 'picture-palaces' from 1906, building up a chain of over fifty by the time of the war. His production company Projektions A. G. Union was founded in 1910.

[11] The founding of the studios at Neubabelsberg dated from 1911, when Guido Seeber, the famous cameraman and one of the chiefs at Bioscop, insisted on new premises. The company purchased considerable space at Babelsberg, allowing some 40,000 square metres for exteriors. The scale of the property as acquired in 1911 was to be a most valuable asset when the studio became later one of the greatest in Europe.

[12] Ernst Lubitsch (1892–1947). Lubitsch worked in Germany until 1922, when he emigrated to the United States.

[13] Emil Jannings (1884–1950). Worked from 1914 with Reinhardt. A friend of Lubitsch, he first appeared in Lubitsch's comedy series in 1917. He had been on the stage from the age of ten.

[14] Pola Negri (b. 1897). Born in Warsaw, she came to Germany in 1916. Her real name was Appolonia Chalupetz. Initially a dancer, she was discovered at the age of fifteen. Lubitsch at first resisted employing her, but was induced to cast her as Carmen after tests.

[15] Henryk Galeen (1892–1949). A Dutchman, he later went to the United States.

[16] Erich Pommer (1889–1966). Son of a business man, had initially managed a French distribution company in Germany, Eclair. He became head of Decla. He had been a producer since 1915. He emigrated to the United States in 1934, working also in Britain with Charles Laughton, with whom he founded the company Mayflower Films. During the 1950s he returned officially to produce films in Germany.

[17] Fritz Lang (b. 1890). Had studied art in Vienna, Munich and Paris. His career in Germany lasted until 1933; he worked in Hollywood 1936–58, after which he returned to direction in Germany.

[18] Fritz Kortner (1892–1970). One of the greatest of Germany's stage actors and directors, having worked with Jessner. An Austrian Jew, he wrote scripts in the U.S. during the Hitler regime, returning to the German stage after the war.

[19] Gustav Ucicky (1898–1961). Began his film career as a cameraman working for Sascha in Vienna.

[20] Mihály Kertész (Michael Curtiz, 1888–1962). Made thirty-eight films in Hungary before leaving for Austria. Worked in Sweden before going to the United States in 1927.

[21] Alexander Korda (1893–1956). A journalist who turned director, first in Hungary and later in Vienna and Berlin, before going to the United States.

CHAPTER TWO pages 11 – 49

[1] During the earlier stages of inflation the price of admission in a typical Berlin cinema rose from 21 to 10,000 marks. In August 1922 the $ stood at 1,250 marks; in July 1923 it rose from 160,000 to 760,000, and in November to 4·2 billion. From 1918 to 1920, the number of cinemas in Germany had grown from 2,299 to 3,731. After stabilization the growth slowed at first: 1925, 3,878; then rose rapidly again: 1927, 4,462 cinemas; 1929, 5,078, or 30 seats per 1,000 population.

[2] Key statistics for the 1920s in feature production were: 1921, 646 films; 1922, 474; 1923, 347; 1924, 271; 1925, 228.

[3] Titles include *Lost Daughters, Hyenas of Lust, A Man's Girlhood*. Among the many public protests was one from the boy scouts of Leipzig. Some of the protests identified pornography with the Jews; the protests were anti-Semitic.

[4] In his *Unsterblicher Film* (vol. I) Heinrich Fraenkel criticizes 'some profound books relating those few films to the mysteries of the German soul and even the aberrations of German foreign policy and the sins of the Gestapo'. He adds that 'Herr Hinz and Fräulein Kunz' – equivalent of 'Tom, Dick and Harry' – 'while presumably the real experts in the mysteries of the German soul would have been hardly aware of such significantly revealing films unless straying into a West End cinema of the few big cities where they could be seen.'

[5] The film, sponsored by Erich Pommer of Decla, was shelved after its completion for lack of a suitable outlet. It achieved its screening at the Marmorhaus (Marble House) in Berlin only through an accident, when another film had fallen through; the Marmorhaus had originally turned it down. It was an immediate success with the intellectuals. Special publicity put it over: posters asked: 'Wo ist Caligari?' 'Du musst Caligari werden', and so forth. The film cost the equivalent of $18,000.

Pommer had passed the original script by Mayer and Janowitz to his associate Rudolf Meinert, a rosy-cheeked type of businessman, who admitted later to Heinrich Fraenkel that he saw it as a 'queer' subject which could be brought into line with the fashionable expressionism and made for a budget of something like £1,000. It was shot in the old, diminutive Weissensee Lixi Studio. When the designers Warm, Reimann and Röhrig turned in their sketches Meinert thought they might have gone too far, but Pommer gave the instruction to go ahead. *Caligari's* predecessor had been *From Morn to Midnight*, adapted from Georg Kaiser's play. Its sets by Robert Neppach were no less expressionistic than those of *Caligari*. But *From Morn to Midnight*, financed by the script-writer Herbert Juttke's father, was never shown in the cinemas, though it enjoyed great success, strangely, in Japan, and recouped there its very modest production costs of a few hundred pounds.

⁶ Carl Mayer (1894–1944). Mayer scripted many of the finest films made in Germany, including *Sylvester*, *The Last Laugh* and *Tartuffe*, as well as *Sunrise* for Murnau in the United States. After 1933 he lived in England, working on occasion with Paul Rotha.

⁷ Conrad Veidt (1893–1943). Initially a stage actor with Reinhardt, he featured in many of the great German films of the 1920s. He left Germany in 1933, working in France, England and the United States. He dropped dead on a Beverley Hills golf course at the age of fifty.

⁸ Werner Krauss (1884–1959). A brilliant stage actor who was to feature in many important films of the 1920s. He supported the Nazi régime, and starred in the anti-Semitic film, *Jud Süss*.

⁹ Robert Wiene (1881–1938) came to films from the theatre. He had previously worked for Messter. After completing his other expressionist films, *Genuine* and *The Hands of Orlac*, he went over to more commercial work. He emigrated to France in 1933, dying in Paris while working with Stroheim on *Ultimatum*.

¹⁰ Two of the designers, Warm and Röhrig, were to have considerable careers as set designers. Reimann did not.

¹¹ Wiene went on to make *Raskolnikov* and a religious film, *I.N.R.I.* (1923) in which Henny Porten played Mary, Werner Krauss Pilate, and Asta Nielsen Mary Magdalen. Grigory Chmara was Christ.

¹² Thea von Harbou (1888–1954). Two years older than Lang, she wrote best-sellers. She supported Hitler, and was later to script two premier Nazi films—*Der Herrscher* and *Jugend*.

¹³ Lang was always accused of going wildly over his budget. He told Heinrich Fraenkel that he never spent more than 5 million marks, and he was prepared to sue UFA for defamation if they encouraged the rumours he had spent up to 8 million. The picture had taken 310 shooting days and

60 nights; there were as many as 750 minor roles, and some 36,000 extras appeared in the mass-spectacle scenes. The film took 17 months to produce. For the Tower of Babel sequence Lang used 1,100 bald men, collected from the dole-queues of the unemployed prepared to sacrifice their hair for money; 150 hairdressers shaved their skulls. Heinrich Fraenkel visited both the *Siegfried* and *Metropolis* sets. Lang, wearing plus-fours, a silk shirt and monocle, directed before the press *con brio*. By the time *Metropolis* was in its final stages, UFA was in dire straits financially. Paramount and MGM put in some 17 million marks, in return for winning a lucrative outlet in Europe. Eventually in 1927 Hugenberg and Ludwig Klitzsch took over management, and UFA's capital was raised to 45 million marks, with backing by the Deutsche Bank. Total assets rose to 57·9 m. marks; policy became highly nationalistic. See page 67.

[14] Written for Roger Manvell, editor of *Penguin Film Review* in 1946.

[15] Wilhelm Dieterle (b. 1893) was one of Reinhardt's actors and appeared in many films before emigrating to the United States in 1930. His first notable film as both director and star was *Menschen am Wege* (1923), in which Marlene Dietrich co-starred.

[16] Paul Leni (1885–1929). After directing films in Germany from 1918 including *Hintertreppe* (1921), Leni went to the United States in 1927, where he directed a number of films, including *The Cat and the Canary, The Man who Laughs*, and *The Last Warning* before his sudden death.

[17] F. W. Murnau (1889–1931) was a stage producer for Reinhardt. After directing his most celebrated film in Germany, *The Last Laugh*, he left in 1926 for the United States. He was meticulous, dictatorial and endlessly thorough. *Nosferatu* was Galeen's first work as a script-writer; it was adapted from Bram Stoker's book (1896), and the film was made out of copyright. Hamilton Deane dramatized the story in 1924 within copyright; Universal later bought the rights afresh, and Bela Lugosi starred in the American *Dracula* (1931), the first of the Dracula cycle.

[18] *Index to the Films of F. W. Murnau*, British Film Institute, 1948.

[19] Ernö Metzner, a well-established art-director, who, for example, designed the sets for Czerépy's film *Alt Heidelberg* (1923).

[20] Arzen von Czerépy (1881–1944).

[21] Notable films using historical backgrounds for spectacle were: 1921–23, *Danton* and *Peter the Great* (Dmitri Buchowetzki); 1922–23, *Lucrezia Borgia* and *Lady Hamilton* (Richard Oswald); 1923, *Wilhelm Tell* (Rudolf Dworsky); 1923, *Fridericus Rex* (Czerépy); 1923, *Helen of Troy* (Manfred Noa); 1927,

Maria Stuart (Leopold Jessner); 1928, *Martin Luther* (Hans Keyser); 1928, *Waterloo* (Karl Grune).

[22] Ludwig Berger (1892–1969). Between his many productions in Germany, Berger worked in Hollywood, where he made relatively undistinguished films, such as *Playboy of Paris*. With the coming of Hitler, he emigrated to England, where he made *The Thief of Bagdad* for Korda, starring Conrad Veidt. He returned to Germany after the war, but did little work in films.

[23] *Index to the Films of F. W. Murnau*, British Film Institute, 1948.

[24] Leopold Jessner (1878–1945) was head of the Berlin State Theatre and second only to Reinhardt as a progressive director in the German theatre; his interest lay in the *avant-garde*.

[25] Lupu Pick (1886–1931). Of Roumanian origin, he died at the age of forty-five after making further films (including *Napoleon on St Helena*, scripted by Abel Gance) which were below the standard set by those he made with Mayer. According to Carl Vincent, *The Last Laugh* should have been the third film in a trilogy starting with *Shattered* and *Sylvester*, but they differed over the exact nature of the character to be given to the hotel doorman.

[26] Karl Grune (1885–1962) came from Reinhardt's theatre.

[27] Paul Czinner (b. 1890). Of Hungarian origin. After the coming of Hitler, Czinner finally emigrated with his wife, Elisabeth Bergner, and settled in Britain.

[28] Ewald A. Dupont (1891–1956). One of the first film critics in Germany, writing from 1911. Made *Piccadilly* in Britain in 1929. From 1943 in the United States.

[29] Georg W. Pabst (1885–1967). A stage actor from the age of fifteen, he came to cinema from direction in the theatre.

[30] According to Paul Rotha in *The Film Till Now*, the film was shot in thirty-four sixteen-hour days, and had a length of 10,000 feet. The version shown in France was cut by 2,000 feet (half-an-hour), all the street scenes being cut. In Russia, the butcher became the murderer instead of the girl. In Britain it was shown only by the London Film Society; in the United States not at all.

[31] Krauss is said to have been unwilling to play the part at first; his father had killed his mother with a knife. See the biographical article on Pabst by Herbert G. Luft, *Films and Filming*, April 1967.

[32] Pabst was later to show Heinrich Fraenkel a photostat of a letter from Ehrenburg confirming that he had no objections to the changes. He received an additional fee of 6,000 marks in compensation.

[33] Arnold Fanck (b. 1889) a former geologist and alpinist, made many films on alpine subjects, including *Wonder of the Ski* (1920) and *The Holy Mountain* (1927).

[34] Walter Ruttmann (1887–1941), abstract painter and experimental film-maker, had made insets for *Siegfried* and for Toller's play *Hoppla!* in the theatre.

[35] See Manvell and Huntley, *The Technique of Film Music*, p. 24, for further comment on the score for *Berlin*.

[36] Lotte Reiniger (b. 1899). Worked on silhouette films in Germany until her emigration to Britain in 1936. She finally settled in London in 1950.

CHAPTER THREE pages 50 – 64

[1] Among the early experimentalists with sound was Oskar Fischinger (1900–67), who designed abstract mobile patterns to established music, as in Brahms' *Hungarian Dance no. 6*. For a full account of his work and films see *Distribution Catalogue*, British Film Institute, 1969, p. 158.

[2] An entirely separate version of this film was produced in England with the title *Sunshine Susie* (1931), featuring Jack Hulbert. For a full analysis of the famous sequence in *Congress Dances* in which Lilian Harvey, as the shop girl, rides in her carriage to the bedroom in the Prince's palace, *see* Manvell and Huntley, *The Technique of Film Music*, pp. 32–4.

[3] Josef von Sternberg (b. 1894). Born in Vienna, he went to New York in childhood, but was constantly living both in Europe and the United States, entering the film industry there before the First World War and working in all branches. Directed *The Salvation Hunters* (1925) from his own script.

[4] Peter Lorre (1904–64). Born in Hungary, Lorre began his career as a stage actor. His principal career was to be in the United States where he went in 1935. He played in Hitchcock's *The Man Who Knew Too Much* in Britain in 1934.

[5] Fedor Ozep (1895–1948) left Russia in 1929; there he had scripted the expressionist film, *Aelita*. Later he worked in France and the United States.

[6] A lengthy reappraisal of this film by Alan Stanbrook appeared in *Films and Filming*, April 1961. Another analysis can be found in Rotha's book *Celluloid*, 1931.

[7] Leni Riefenstahl (b. 1902) began her career as a dancer. She first appeared in Fanck's film *Der Heilige Berg* (1926).

[8] Max Ophüls (1902–57). Originally an actor and stage producer, Ophüls

worked in France, 1933–41, and then in the United States. He returned to France in 1950.

[9] *Cinema Quarterly*, Summer 1933.

[10] For a study of the evolution of the idea for the character of the universal destroyer in Lang's film, see the perceptive article by John Russell Taylor, 'The Nine Lives of Dr Mabuse' in *Sight and Sound*, Winter, 1961–62.

CHAPTER FOUR pages 65 – 74

[1] See the authors' book, *Doctor Goebbels* (1960), Chapter V.

[2] The successive Presidents of the Reichsfilmkammer under Goebbels, as President of the whole cultural machine, were Dr Fritz Scheuermann, an economist (1933–35), S.S. Oberführer Professor Oswald Lehnich, a political economist (1935–39), and finally a film producer-director, Professor Carl Froelich, who stayed in control until the régime collapsed. The corresponding heads of the Ministry's film department were Dr Ernst Saeger (1933–37), Wolfgang Fischer (1937–38), Ernst Lichtenstern (1938–39), Dr Franz Hippler (1939–43)—later to be director of *The Eternal Jew*—Dr Peter Gast (1943–44), Kurt Parbel (1944) and Hans Hinkel (1944–45), a virulent Nazi who had been a member of the Party since 1921.

[3] It was closed in 1940 on account of the war.

[4] Hans Albers, whose girl-friend Hansi Burg was Jewish and living in England, supported her throughout the Hitler period by subsidies from his work in Sweden, money acquired outside the German currency regulations. They eventually married after the war.

[5] Attendance in 1935 was some 304 million, or 5·9 attendance per head of population; in 1942 it was over 1,000 million, or 14·3 per head of population.

CHAPTER FIVE pages 75 – 98

[1] Leni Riefenstahl preceded her better-known film with a shorter one of the same subject, *Sieg des Glaubens* (*Victory of Faith*, 1933), derived from the 1933 Party Congress.

[2] For background articles on the Nazi cinema see *Cinema Quarterly*, Summer 1935, *World Film News*, September 1936; post-war, *Sight and Sound*, Autumn 1955, Autumn 1963, and *Films and Filming*, April 1966. During 1968–69 a brilliant series of half-hour television programmes was produced in Germany under the title *Film im Dritten Reich*, made up of extracts derived from the principal story feature films of the period. They were presented with such theme titles as: 'The Führer against Democracy', 'Distortion of the Weimar

Republic', 'You are Nothing—the People are Everything', 'Marxism—Germany's Arch Enemy', 'Blood and Soil', 'From the Nation to the Army', 'Perfidious Albion', 'Anti-Semitism', and so forth. During 1970 the National Film Theatre in London presented for the first time since the War a series of programmes representing a comprehensive selection of films made under the Nazis. The programme was prepared by a special committee set up by the British Film Institute and made up largely of historians and other specialists.

3 Leni Riefenstahl herself published a book about the making of the film—*Hinter den Kulissen des Reichparteitag Films* (1935)—in which she claimed that the preparations for the Congress were made with a view to her film.

4 See Manvell and Fraenkel, *Dr Goebbels*, Chapter V.

5 Conrad Veidt was to appear in the British production which was based on the book—*Jew Süss* (1933).

6 This film was used as the main indictment against Veit Harlan during his trial in Hamburg in 1950 on charges of crimes against humanity. He was acquitted. With regard to the British film, directed by Lothar Mendes, Heinrich Fraenkel remembers a conversation he had with Conrad Veidt on the telephone to Germany. Veidt refused to discuss coming to Britain to play the part in case his phone was tapped, and negotiations were eventually conducted in an hour-long phone conversation between H.F. and Mendes at Shepherd's Bush studios and Veidt in Prague. His acceptance of the part meant he could never return to Germany while Hitler was in power.

7 Account should be taken of the fearful 'record' films taken by Nazi staff cameramen—for example, in the Warsaw Ghetto, or, in 1944 after the failure of the attempt on Hitler's life, the hanging of the 'guilty' army officers. See Manvell and Fraenkel, *The July Plot*, p, 198.

8 For an examination of a considerable cross-section of German educational cinema during the Nazi period see *Report on German Educational Films* (British Film Institute, 1946). Also 'The Use of Visual Aids in German Schools', by G. Buckland Smith, *Sight and Sound*, Winter 1945–46.

9 The International Olympic Committee gave Leni Riefenstahl the exclusive rights to cover the Games, and the German government had no specific power to prevent this. Consequently, Goebbels did his best to hinder the facilities available to the technicians in the same fashion as he had sought to sabotage the filming of the Nuremberg Congress. Once more, however, pits were dug for the cameras, tracks were laid for travelling shots, shots

were taken from mobile cranes and from cars travelling at speed. Cameras were specially designed for underwater shooting. In all, a million feet of film were shot, representing some 500 hours' running-time. The editing took eighteen months. The film was awarded the Grand Prix at the 1938 Venice Film Festival. Leni Riefenstahl received awards from the French, Swedish and Greek governments, and, post-war, a diploma and gold medal from the International Olympic Committee, who had commissioned the film in the first place. Even Stalin sent a letter of praise!

Leni Riefenstahl completed a further film during the war—*Tiefland*, which was finally released in 1954. In this she played a gypsy girl with whom a Spanish shepherd is in love. The film returns to the atmosphere of *The Blue Light*, and was shot in the Italian Alps under her direction. Subsequently she was to work in Africa, attempting, though short of money, to make a documentary on the slave trade in East Africa in 1956, and acting as camera-woman to an expedition in Sudan, Kenya and Tanganyika in 1964, where she obtained some remarkable photographs of the little-known Nuba tribe, with whom she lived for several months.

CHAPTER SIX pages 99 – 113

[1] Among the German actors and film-makers put under temporary arrest for their Party affiliations or debarred from working for a short while were Werner Krauss, Heinrich George, Gustav Gründgens, the director Karl Ritter, and Emil Jannings. On the other hand Paul Wegener received an honorary degree from Rostock University in East Germany for his stand against Nazism. Leni Riefenstahl was permitted to resume her career after clearance in the French Zone.

[2] *The Incomparable Crime* (1967). In the last chapter of this book the authors give a much fuller account of the problems, moral, political and economic, which faced post-war Germany.

[3] Statistics for 1947 give 1,007 cinemas in British Zone, 700 in U.S. Zone, 1,400 in Russian Zone. The total for all Germany appeared to be between 3,000 and 3,500, as compared with 7,000 before the bombing.

[4] Heinrich Fraenkel himself viewed officially during 1944–45 a large number of captured German feature films in Britain with a view to recommending those suitable for general showing. Barely half-a-dozen out of about a hundred were recommended to be forbidden.

See also article by H. H. Wollenberg, *Sight and Sound*, Spring 1946.

[5] The late Dr H. H. Wollenberg was a friend of both authors. A prominent

film journalist in Berlin during the 1920s and early 1930s, he became a Jewish refugee to this country, where he served as an air raid warden during the war. He became an associate editor of *Penguin Film Review* (1946–49). He was the author of *Fifty Years of German Film* (1948).

[6] Erich Pommer, who attended the première of this film in the uniform of an American general, sat next to Heinrich Fraenkel, and told him that in Hildegard Knef there were the makings of an international star.

[7] The same theme was developed less effectively in an American-licensed German film, *Between Yesterday and Tomorrow* (*Zwischen Gestern und Morgen*, 1947), directed by Harald Braun. This film became confused, with too many flash-backs and a sub-plot involving the recovery of a lost piece of jewellery.

[8] Käutner told Heinrich Fraenkel of the difficulty he had with the British authorities to be allowed to film a single bullet shot through the windscreen of the car. Eventually he was permitted to have his single gun-shot, in a gymnasium. No German was allowed firearms in those days. The film won an award at the Locarno Film Festival of 1948, and Hildegard Neff received the award as the best actress.

[9] Otto Normalverbraucher, meaning Otto living-off-the-normal-calory-intake. Shortly after the release of this film the currency reform was introduced, bringing the end of semi-starvation for the average German.

[10] For a full account see 'The German Film Institute' by G. Buckland-Smith, *Sight and Sound* (Summer 1947); the author was Film Officer to the Control Commission in Hamburg. Roger Manvell accompanied Paul Rotha and others to Hamburg in 1946 to meet the young potential documentary film-makers and discuss ideas for this sort of work.

[11] His extraordinary career during and after the Nazi régime is most movingly told in an interview with Geoffrey Boswall of BBC-TV in the *Journal of the Society of Film and Television Arts*, Summer/Autumn 1968.

CHAPTER SEVEN pages 114 – 123

[1] 4·5 m.DM, 1951–52; 7 m.DM, 1952–53; 11 m.DM, 1953–54; 14·5 m.DM, 1954–55; and 15·5 m.DM in 1962–63. Production costs, which were on average 850,000 DM in 1954, rose by the end of the decade to well over the million mark. Production figures in the later 1950s were: 1955, 124; 1959, 106.

[2] *Sight and Sound*, Summer 1956.

[3] There seems to be little evidence that this was really so. See Manvell and Fraenkel, *Heinrich Himmler*.

⁴ Pabst's own explanation to Heinrich Fraenkel was that he felt forced to return home in spite of the Nazis (whom he loathed). He loved Austria, and his comfortable estate. Once there, he turned down far more films than the ones he made. 'I was too busy surviving,' he said.

⁵ For the full details, see Luft's article in *Films and Filming*, April 1967. Pabst was for a while involved in Dino de Laurentiis's production of *Ulysses*. The facts given in this section owe much to Herbert G. Luft's article.

⁶ Pabst's film appeared simultaneously with another production on the same subject, an inferior film, *20 Juli*, directed by Falk Harnack; this film implied that the *coup d'état* represented the will of the whole people, which it emphatically did not.

⁷ *Unbewältigte Vergangenheit*, the German term for the difficulty in accepting the full implication of the Nazi conspiracy for power and the crimes committed by the régime.

⁸ Staudte's other films for DEFA were *Die Seltsamen Abenteuer des Herrn Fridolin B.* (1948), and *Rotation* (1949).

CHAPTER EIGHT pages 124 – 133

¹ The number of cinemas in the Federal Republic halved during the decade, dropping from some 7,000 to 3,500. Cinemas were still closing in 1970, and audiences declined further in 1967 and 1968 by eighteen per cent, from 234 million to 192 million, or less than four million a week.

² Leiser was later to return to Germany, where he became for a while joint director of the Berlin Film and Television Academy.

³ Nazi film records, like surviving documents of the régime, were either captured or confiscated at the end of the war. Since 1958 this material has been gradually returned to Germany—the Russians giving such records and films as they choose to the East German Central Archives Office in Potsdam, and the Western Allies depositing the records in their possession with the Bundesarchiv in Koblenz.

⁴ The film industry in Germany delights in fanciful erotic titles, which it attaches even to its imports. *The Touchables* became *Between Bed and Beat*, *The Girl with the Motorcycle* became *Naked under Leather*, while *Lover Come Back* became *A Pair of Pyjamas for Two*.

Bibliography

AMENGUAL, BARTHELEMY, *G. W. Pabst*. Paris, Seghers. 1966.

BARTHEL, W. and SCHMIDT, H., *Der Junge Deutsche Film*. Dokumentation der Constantin Film. Munich, 1967.

BAUER, ALFRED, *The Tendentious Feature Films in Germany (1933–45)*. Unpublished, Berlin, 1947.

BAXTER, JOHN, *Science Fiction in the Cinema*. London, Zwemmer. 1970.

BECKER, LUTZ, *The Cinema in Nazi Germany*. Department of Film, Slade College of Art. 1969 (unpublished).

BERGER, LUDWIG, *Wir sind vom gleichen Stoff aus dem die Träume sind*. Tübingen, Rainer Wunderlich Verlag. 1953.

BORDE, RAYMOND, BUACHE, FREDDY, and COURTADE, FRANCIS, *Le Cinéma Réaliste Allemand*. Lyon, SERDOC. 1965.

BRAMSTED, ERNEST, K., *Goebbels and National Socialist Propaganda 1925–45*. Michigan State University Press. 1965.

BUACHE, FREDDY, *G. W. Pabst*. Lyon, SERDOC. 1965.

BUCHER, FELIX, *Germany: an Illustrated Guide*. Screen Series. London, Zwemmer; New York, A. S. Barnes. 1971.

COURTADE, FRANCIS, *Jeune Cinéma Allemand*. Lyon, SERDOC, Premier Plan. 1969.

DEFA, *20 Jahre DEFA-Spielfilm*. Berlin, Henschelverlag. 1968.

EISNER, LOTTE, *F. W. Murnau*. Paris, Le Terrain Vague. 1964. *The Haunted Screen*. London, Thames and Hudson. 1969. (Translated from *L'Ecran Démoniaque*. Paris, Encyclopédie du Cinéma, 1952.)

FRAENKEL, HEINRICH, *Unsterblicher Film*, Vol. I, 1955; Vol. II, 1957. Munich, Kindler.

FÜRSTENAU, THEO, *Wandlungen im Film (Junge Deutsche Produktion)*. Biebrich, Deutsches Institut für Filmkunde. N.D. (1968).

HALL, DAVID STEURT, *Film in the Third Reich*. University of California Press. 1969.

HEIDBÜCHEL, JACOB, *Neuer Deutscher Film: Eine Dokumentation.* Verband der Deutschen Filmclubs, Mannheim. 1967.

HEMBUS, JOE, *Der Deutsche Film kann garnicht besser sein.* Bremen, Schünemann Verlag. 1961.

HEMPEL, ROLF, *Carl Mayer.* Berlin, Henschelverlag. 1968.

HERLTH, ROBERT, *Filmarchitektur.* Munich, Deutsches Institut für Film und Fernsehen. 1965.

HIBBIN, NINA, *Eastern Europe: An Illustrated Guide.* Screen Series. London, Zwemmer. 1970 (for section on East German cinema).

JEANNE, RENÉ, and FORD, CHARLES, *Histoire Encyclopédique du Cinéma 1895–1929.* Paris, S.E.D.E., 1953.

JENSEN, PAUL M., *The Cinema of Fritz Lang.* London and New York, International Film Guide Series. 1969.

KLAUE, WOLFGANG (Editor), *Filme contra Faschismus.* Berlin, Staatliches Filmarchiv der D.D.R. 1964.

KNIETZSCH, HORST, *Film Gestern und Heute.* Leipzig, Urania Verlag. 1963.

KRACAUER, SIEGFRIED, *From Caligari to Hitler.* London, Dobson. 1947.

KURTZ, RUDOLF, *Expressionismus im Film.* Berlin, Wolffsohn. 1925.

LEISER, ERWIN, *Deutschland Erwache (Propaganda im Film des 3. Reiches).* Hamburg, Rowohlt Taschenbuch. 1968.

LONDON, KURT, *Film Music.* London, Faber and Faber. 1936.

MANVELL, ROGER (Editor), *Experiment in the Film.* London, Grey Walls Press. 1949. (Includes article, 'Avant-garde Film in Germany', by Hans Richter.)

MANVELL, ROGER, and FRAENKEL, HEINRICH, *Dr Goebbels.* London, Heinemann. 1960.

MAYER, CARL, *Sylvester. A Screenplay: translated into Italian.* Venice, Marsilio, for Venice Film Festival, 1967.

MUSÉE DU CINÉMA, BRUXELLES, *Fantastique et Réalisme dans le Cinéma Allemand 1912–33.* Brussels, Musée du Cinéma, 1969.

NARATH, DR ALBERT, *Oskar Messter.* Berlin, Deutsche Kinemathek e V. 1966.

PLEYER, PETER, *Deutscher Nachkriegs Film 1946–47.* Münster, Verlag C. J. Fahle GMBH. 1965.

RIEFENSTAHL, LENI, *Hinter den Kulissen des Reichsparteitag-Films,* Munich, Zentralverlag der NSDAP. 1935.

ROTHA, PAUL, *The Film Till Now*. London, Cape. 1930 (Revised, with Richard Griffith; London, Vision, 1949.)

SADOUL, GEORGES, *Histoire Générale du Cinéma*, Vols. I et seq. Paris, Denoël. 1947, etc.

VENICE FILM FESTIVAL, *Il Cinema nel Movimento Espressionista Tedesco e la Figura di Carl Mayer*. 1967.

VINCENT, CARL, *Histoire de L'Art Cinématographique*. Brussels, Trident. n.d.

WOLLENBERG, H. H., *Fifty Years of German Cinema*. London, Falcon Press. 1948.

ZEMAN, Z. A. B., *Nazi Propaganda*. Oxford University Press. 1964.

Index of principal names

Roman numerals are page numbers in the list of illustrations

Select index of films

(German titles are given only where there is no English one)

Numbers in italics refer to plates

158